STUDY NOTES

SSC

Quantitative Aptitude

VOLUME - 3

QUANTITATIVE APTITUDE

TABLE OF CONTENT

DISCOUNT

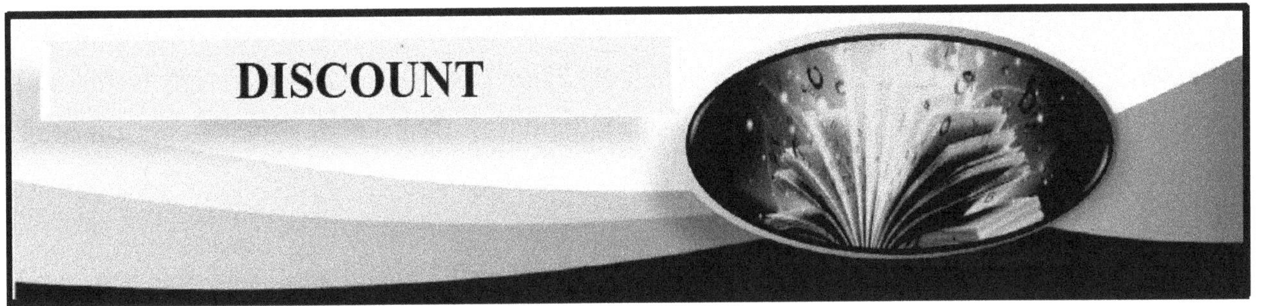

Introduction

A discount is a price reduction that is offered to customers on a product or service. Discounts are a common marketing tool used by businesses to encourage customers to purchase their products or services. Discounts can take many different forms, such as a percentage off the regular price, a fixed amount off the price, or a buy-one-get-one-free offer.

Discounts are used for various purposes, including attracting new customers, retaining existing ones, clearing out inventory, or simply increasing sales volume. For example, a business may offer a discount to new customers as an incentive to try their products or services, or offer discounts to existing customers to reward their loyalty and encourage repeat business.

Discounts can also be used to clear out excess inventory or seasonal products, such as discounted winter clothing at the end of the winter season. Additionally, discounts can be used to increase sales volume during slow periods, such as offering discounts during the off-season for travel or tourism.

Discounts can be offered for a limited time only, such as during a holiday or special event, or they can be ongoing promotions that are available year-round. For example, many businesses offer discounts to seniors, military personnel, or students year-round to attract these specific customer demographics.

While discounts can be an effective marketing tool, it's important for businesses to carefully consider the impact on their bottom line. Offering too many discounts can lead to reduced profit margins, and may even devalue the perceived quality of the product or service being offered. Therefore, businesses should strike a balance between offering attractive discounts and maintaining profitability.

In summary, discounts are a common marketing tool used by businesses to encourage customers to purchase their products or services. They can take many different forms and are used for various purposes, but businesses must carefully consider the impact on their profitability when offering discounts.

Profit, Loss, and Discount are one of the most frequently asked topics in the SSC and Railways Exams. It is asked in the Quantitative Aptitude Section in most of the SSC & Railways exams. This will help the aspirants in understanding the most critical concepts of Profit, Loss, and Discount. It will also give the SSC aspirants a glimpse into the kind of questions that have been asked in previous years' examinations and the ones that are expected to be asked most frequently.

Profit, Loss, and Discount are crucial from the perspective of competitive government exams such as Staff Selection Commission (SSC) and Railways as it is highly scoring and takes very little time to solve questions under this topic.

Important Concept

Cost Price (CP)	Money paid by the shopkeeper to acquire goods from the manufacturer.
Selling Price (SP)	Price at which the goods are sold to the buyers. It can be a discounted or a marked-up price.
Profit	Whenever the shopkeeper gains on selling a product, he is said to have made a profit on it. It is calculated by deducting CP from SP, and the answer is always a positive figure.
Loss	Whenever a shopkeeper loses on selling a product, he is said to "have incurred a loss. It is also incurred by deducting CP from SP. However, the answer is always a negative figure.
Marked Price (MP)	A shopkeeper almost always knows that his buyers are going to bargain with him. He, therefore, marks up his Cost Price to leave some buffer zone for reducing it when the customer bargains. Marked Price = Cost Price + Mark up.
Discount	This is a concession given by the seller to the buyer. It is an amount that reduces the marked price and gives us the selling price. Discount = Marked Price - Selling Price.

Terms Of Discount

In finance, the term "discount" refers to a reduction in the price or value of an asset, liability, or investment. Here are some terms related to discounts:

1. Discount rate: The discount rate is the interest rate used to discount future cash flows to their present value. It is commonly used in discounted cash flow analysis to determine the value of an investment or asset.
2. Face value: The face value is the nominal or original value of a financial instrument, such as a bond or a bill of exchange, which is often different from its market value.
3. Par value: The par value is the value assigned to a stock or bond at the time of issuance, which is often used as a reference for calculating the dividend or interest payments.
4. Market value: The market value is the current price at which an asset or security is traded in the market.
5. Discounted cash flow (DCF): Discounted cash flow is a financial analysis technique used to estimate the value of an investment or asset by discounting future cash flows to their present value.
6. Discount period: The discount period is the period during which a buyer is allowed to pay a lower price for a product or service, often due to a promotional offer or a bulk purchase.
7. Trade discount: A trade discount is a reduction in the price of a product or service offered to a specific group of customers, such as wholesalers or retailers.
8. Cash discount: A cash discount is a reduction in the price of a product or service offered to customers who pay their bills promptly, usually within a specified period.

FUNDAMENTAL OF DISCOUNT

The fundamental concept of discount is that the value of money decreases over time due to inflation, opportunity cost, and other factors. As a result, a dollar received today is worth more than a dollar received in the future. Discounts are used in finance and accounting to adjust the present value of future payments or receipts.

Discounts can be applied to various financial instruments, such as bonds, bills of exchange, and promissory notes. The discount is usually expressed as a percentage of the face value of the instrument, and the resulting discounted value represents the present value of the future cash flows associated with the instrument.

The process of discounting involves using a discount rate, which is typically the prevailing interest rate or a rate of return that represents the opportunity cost of investing the money elsewhere. The discount rate is used to calculate the present value of future cash flows by discounting them back to the present time. The formula for calculating the present value of a future payment using a discount rate is:

Present value = Future value / (1 + discount rate)^n

Where:

- Future value is the value of the payment to be received in the future.
- A discount rate is the rate used to discount the future value to the present value.
- n is the number of periods between the present time and the time when the payment is received.

Discounts are used in many financial transactions, such as loans, investments, and sales. For example, a borrower may receive a loan at a discounted interest rate, or a seller may offer a discount to a buyer who pays cash instead of using credit. Understanding the fundamentals of discounting is essential for making informed financial decisions and evaluating the true value of financial instruments.

Tips and Tricks

- CP if gain % is given:
  $\text{CP} = (100/(100 + \text{ gain }\%)) * \text{SP}$
- CP if loss % is given:
  $\text{CP} = (100/(100 - \text{loss }\%)) * \text{SP}$
- SP if gain % is given:
  $\text{SP} = ((100 + \text{ gain }\%)/100) * \text{CP}$
- SP if loss % is given:
  $\text{SP} = ((100 - \text{losS }\%)/100) * \text{CP}$
- Profit % = (Profit/ CP) * 100
- Loss % = (Loss / CP) * 100
- If there is no discount, then Marked Price must be assumed equivalent to Selling Price. In that case, MP = SP
- Discount % = (Discount / Marked Price) * 100

- If there are two discounts given successively, then the total discount given is ($x + y - x * y/100$)
- If the Cost Price of articles 'a' is equal to the Selling Price of articles 'b', what is the resultant percentage of profit or the percentage of loss? $(b - a)/b * 100$

Example of Discount

1. A shopkeeper is about to sell some goods, and he anticipates that there will be at least 45/2 gain per cent on this Cost Price. If he can sell the product for Rs. 392, calculate his Profit.

Solution:

Substitute all the values in this formula - CP = (100/ (100 + gain %)) * SP

C.P. comes out to be Rs. 320.

Profit = SP – CP = 392 – 320 = Rupees 72.

2. A shopkeeper sold a bag at a loss of 5%. He sold it for Rs. 1140. Calculate at what price the bag should be sold so that he has a 5% profit.

Solution:

(100 – loss %)/ First Selling Price = (100 + gain %)/ Second Selling Price

Substitute all the figures in the above-mentioned formula.

95/1140 = 105/x

x = 1260

The new Selling Price should be Rupees 1260.

3. A shopkeeper wants to earn a profit of 8%, and he fixes the marked price at 35% above the CP. What is the discount % allowed by him to the buyer to earn a profit of 8%?

Solution:

Such questions must be attempted by assuming the value of CP to be 100.

Marked up price becomes 135.

Profit becomes 8.

The Selling Price is 108.

Discount is 135 – 108 = 27

Discount % = (Discount/ Marked Price) * 100

(27/ 135) * 100

=20 %

4. A bag of flour is purchased for Rs. 600. If some portion of the material, say ¼, is sold at 20 % loss and the remaining ¾ is sold at 8 % gain. Calculate the overall percentage of either profit or loss?

Solution:

The first step would be to calculate the Selling Price. This will make the problem easier because if we have SP, we can calculate the gain and loss percentage.

Second step would be to calculate: Money received after ¼ of the material:

(1/ 4) * 600 * (80/ 100) = Rupees 120

The third step would be to calculate: Money received after selling 3/4th of the material.

(3/ 4) * 600 * (110/ 100) = Rupees 495

Now we have the selling price = 495 + 120 = Rupees 615

Profit = SP – CP

615 – 600 = Rupees 15

Profit % = (Profit/ CP) * 100

= (15/600)*100

= 2.5 % is the overall profit percentage.

MULTIPLE CHOICE QUESTIONS

1. Successive discounts of 20% and 10% are equivalent to a single discount of:

A. 15%

B. 28%

C. 25%

D. 30%

Answer: B

Explanation:

Let Price is 100

New price after 20% discount = 80

10% discount on 80 = 8,

Price after both discount = 80-8 =72

Total discount = 100-72 = 28%

Alternate method

20 + 10% of 80 = 28%

Short Trick

Formula for successive discount x and y

$$x + y - \frac{x \times y}{100}\%$$

$$\Rightarrow 20 + 10 - \frac{20 \times 10}{100} = 28\%$$

2. Single discount equivalent to the series of discounts 20%, 10% and 5% is equal to:

A. 32%

B. 30%

C. 30.7%

D. 31.6%

Answer: D

Explanation:

20 + 10% of 80 = 28%

28 + 5% of 72 = 28+3.6 = 31.6%

3. A store has an offer 'Buy 4 Get 1 Free'. What is the net percentage of the discount?

A. 10%
B. 15%
C. 20%
D. 23%

Answer: C
Explanation:
Let price of one item is 100.
Offer Price of 5 items 'Buy 4 Get 1 Free' = 4 + 1 = 400+0 = 400
One item price in offer = 400/5 = 80
Discount = 100 – 80 = 20%

4. A scooter is sold at three successive discounts of 10%, 5% and 2%. If the marked price of the scooter is ₹18,000, find its net selling price.
A. ₹ 15,028.20
B. ₹ 15,082.00
C. ₹ 15,082.20
D. ₹ 15,080.00

Answer: C
Explanation:
Price after 10% discount = 18000 – 1800 = 16200
Price after 5% discount = 16200 – 810 =15390
Price after 2% discount = 15390 – 307.80 =1582.20

5. A sofa-set listed at ₹800 is sold to a retailer at successive discounts of 25% and 15% by the wholesaler. Then the cost price of the sofa-set for retailer is :
A. ₹500
B. ₹510
C. ₹550
D. ₹560

Answer: B
Explanation:

$$800 \times \left(1 - \frac{25}{100}\right) \times \left(1 - \frac{15}{100}\right)$$
$$= 800 \times 0.75 \times 0.85 = 510$$

6. A shopkeeper marks his goods 20% higher than the cost price and allows a discount of 5%. The percentage of his profit is :

A. 15%

B. 20%

C. 10%

D. 14%

Answer: C

Explanation:

Let CP is 100

The marked price is 120.

5% discount on 120 = 6

New Price = 120 – 6 = 114

Profit percentage = 114-100 = 14%

7. The marked price is 20% higher than the cost price. A discount of 20% is given on the market price. By this type of sale, there is :

A. 4% loss

B. 2% loss

C. No loss no gain

D. 4% gain

Answer: A

Explanation:

Gain percentage $= 20 - 20 - \frac{20\times20}{100} = -4\%$

8. A man allows a discount of 10% on a book whose marked price is ₹40. What is the cost price so that the profit is 20%?

A. ₹ 35

B. ₹ 40

C. ₹ 30

D. ₹ 45

Answer: C

Explanation:

120% of CP = 90% of 40

x= 40

9. After allowing 10% discount, a dealer wishes to sell a machine for ₹2700. At what price must the machine be marked?

A. ₹ 2700

B. ₹ 2870

C. ₹ 2460

D. ₹ 3000

Answer: D

Explanation:

90% of CP = 2700

CP = 3000

10. A merchant offers an 8% discount on all his goods and still makes a profit of 15%. If an item is marked ₹ 250, then its cost price is:

A. ₹180

B. ₹200

C. ₹230

D. ₹187

Answer: B

Explanation:

92% of MP = 115% of CP

92 x 250 = 115 x CP

CP = ₹200

11. The marked price of a CD is ₹ 250. It is sold for ₹225. The rate of discount is:

A. 2.5%

B. 10%

C. 25%

D. 11.12%

Answer: B

Explanation:

Discount = 250 – 225 = 25

25 discounts on 250 = 10%

12. A seller gains 20% profit even after allowing 10% discount, if the amount of profit on a TV set is ₹750, then the marked price of the TV set is :

A. ₹ 5200

B. ₹ 5000

C. ₹ 4800

D. ₹ 5500

Answer: B

Explanation:

20% of CP = 750, CP = 3750

90% of Marked Price = 120% of 3750 (CP)

Marked Price = $\frac{3750 \times 120}{90} = 5000$

13. The marked price of an item is twice the cost price. For a gain of 15%, the discount should be:

A. 7.5%

B. 20.5%

C. 32.5%

D. 42.5%

Answer: D

Explanation:

CP is 100 , MP = 200

Selling price for gain of 15% = 115

Discount = 200 – 115 = 85

85 of 200 = 42.5%

14. If a discount of 20% on the marked price of a shirt saves a man ₹150, how much did he pay for the shirt?

A. ₹ 600

B. ₹ 650

C. ₹ 500

D. ₹ 620

Answer: A

Explanation:

Marked price = 100

Price after 20 % discount = 80

Save 20 on 100. Save 1 on 5

save 150 on marked price ₹750.

Pay = 750 -150 =₹600

15. A trader marked the price of his commodity to include a profit of 25%. He allowed a discount of 16% on the market price. His actual profit was.

A. 5%

B. 9%

C. 16%

D. 25%

Answer: A

Explanation:

Cost Price = 100

Marked Price = 125

Selling price 84% of 125 = 105

Profit = 105-100 = 5%

16. A fan is listed at ₹1400, and the discount offered is 10%. What additional discount must be given to bring the net selling price to ₹1200?

A. $16\frac{2}{3}\%$

B. 5%

C. $4\frac{16}{21}\%$

D. 6%

Answer: C

Explanation:

Marked Price = 1400

After 10% discount = 1400 − 140 = 1260

Second discount = 1260 − 1200 = ₹60

Second discount % = $\frac{60\times100}{1260} = 4\frac{16}{21}\%$

17. After allowing a discount of 12% on the marked price of an article, it is sold for Rs.880. Find its marked price.

A. Rs.2,000

B. Rs.1,100

C. Rs.2,100

D. Rs.1,000

Answer: D

Explanation:

Marked price.

$$= \frac{100}{100 - 12} \times 880 = \text{Rs. } 1000$$

18. When a shopkeeper gives 10% discount on the list price of a toy, his gain is 20%. If he had given a discount of 20%, his percentage of gain would have been:

A. $8\frac{1}{3}\%$

B. $6\frac{2}{3}\%$

C. 15%

D. 10%

Answer: B

Explanation:

Let the cost price of toy be Rs. 100 and the marked price be x.

$$\frac{x \times 90}{100} = 120$$

$$x = \frac{120 \times 100}{90} = \text{Rs. } \frac{400}{3}$$

S.P. after a discount of 20%

$$= 80\% \text{ of } \frac{400}{3}$$

$$= \frac{400 \times 80}{300} = \frac{320}{3} = 106\frac{2}{3}$$

Profit percent

$$= 106\frac{2}{3} - 100 = 6\frac{2}{3}\%$$

19. An article is sold at a discount of 20% and an additional discount of 30% is allowed on cash payment. If Vidya purchased the article by paying Rs.2240 in cash, the marked price of the article was:

A. Rs.4368

B. Rs.4000

C. Rs.4480

D. Rs.4400

Answer: B

Explanation:

Let the marked price of the article be x.

Equivalent discount for successive discounts of 30% and 20%

$$= \left(30 + 20 - \frac{30 \times 20}{100}\right)\%$$

$$= (50 - 6)\% = 44\%$$

$$(100 - 44)\% \text{ of } x = 2240$$

$$\frac{x \times 56}{100} = 2240$$

$$x = \frac{2240 \times 100}{56} = \text{Rs. } 4000$$

20. A trader gains 15% after selling an item at a 10% discount on the printed price. The ratio of the cost price and printed price of the item is:

A. 17 : 18

B. 18 : 23

C. 18 : 25

D. 17 : 23

Answer: B

Explanation:

Let the CP of article be x and its marked price be y.

According to the question,

$$90\% \text{ of } y = 115\% \text{ of } x$$

$$\frac{y \times 90}{100} = \frac{x \times 115}{100}$$

$$\frac{x}{y} = \frac{90}{115} = \frac{18}{23} \Rightarrow 18:23$$

Using Rule 6,

Here, r = 15%, D = 10%

$$\frac{MP}{CP} = \frac{100 + r}{100 - D}$$

$$= \frac{100 + 15}{100 - 10}$$

$$\frac{M.P.}{C.P.} = \frac{115}{90}$$

$$\frac{C.P.}{M.P.} = \frac{90}{115}$$

$$\frac{C.P.}{M.P.} = \frac{18}{23}$$

C.P.: M.P. = 18: 23

21. A retailer gets a discount of 40% on the printing price of an article. The retailer sells it at the printing price. His gain per cent is:

A. 55%

B. 40%

C. 75%

D. $66\frac{2}{3}\%$

Answer: D

Explanation:

Let the printed price of the article be Rs. 100

Discount = 40%

C.P. = Rs. (100 – 40) = Rs. 60

S.P. = Rs. 100

$$\text{Gain }\% = \frac{40}{60} \times 100$$

$$= \frac{200}{3} = 66\frac{2}{3}\%$$

22. The selling price of an article is Rs.1,920 and the discount given is 4%. The marked price of the article is:

A. Rs.2,000

B. Rs.2,400

C. Rs.1,200

D. Rs.1,600

Answer: A

Explanation:

If the marked price of the article be x, then.

$$96\% \text{ of } x = 1920$$

$$\frac{x \times 96}{100} = 1920$$

$$x = \frac{1920 \times 100}{96} = \text{Rs. } 2000$$

Using Rule 2,

$$\text{S.P.} = \text{Rs. } 1920 \text{D} = 4\% \text{ M.P.} = ?$$

$$\text{M.P.} = \frac{\text{S.P.} \times 100}{100 - \text{D}}$$

$$= \frac{1920 \times 100}{100 - 4}$$

$$= \frac{1920 \times 100}{96} = \text{Rs. } 2000$$

23. Rahim bought a T.V. with 20% discount on list price. Had he bought it with 25% discount he would have saved Rs.500. At what price did he buy the T.V?

A. Rs. 12,000

B. Rs. 16,000

C. Rs. 8,000

D. Rs. 10,000

Answer: C

Explanation:

If the marked price of T.V. be x, then,

$$\frac{x \times 5}{100} = 500$$

$$x = \frac{500 \times 100}{5} = \text{Rs. } 10000$$

Initial S.P. of T.V.

$$= \frac{10000 \times 80}{100} = \text{Rs. } 8000$$

24. A shopkeeper sells his goods at 15% discount. The marked price of an article whose selling price is Rs.629 is:

A. Rs.704

B. Rs.740

C. Rs.614

D. Rs.700

Answer: B

Explanation:

Let the marked price be x.

$$\frac{x \times 85}{100} = 629$$

$$x = \frac{629 \times 100}{85} = \text{Rs. } 740$$

Using Rule 2,

$$\text{M.P. } = ?, \text{S.P. } = \text{Rs. } 629, D = 15\%$$

$$\text{M.P. } = \frac{\text{S.P. } \times 100}{100 - D}$$

$$= \frac{629 \times 100}{100 - 15}$$

$$= \frac{62900}{85} = \text{Rs. } 740$$

25. A shopkeeper sells his goods at 10% discount on the market price. What price should he mark on an article that costs him Rs.900 to gain 10%?

A. Rs.1250

B. Rs.1275

C. Rs.1100

D. Rs.1175

Answer: C

Explanation:

$$\text{C.P. } = \text{Rs. } 900, \text{Gain } = 10\%$$

$$\text{S.P. } = \text{Rs. } \left(\frac{110}{100} \times 900\right) = \text{Rs. } 990$$

Let the marked price be x.

$$\frac{90}{100}x = 990$$

$$x = \frac{990 \times 100}{90} = \text{Rs. } 1100$$

26. Ravi buys an article with a discount of 25% on its marked price. He makes a profit of 10% by selling it at Rs.660. The marked price of the article was:

A. Rs.700

B. Rs.600

C. Rs.685

D. Rs.800

Answer: D

Explanation:

CP of the article for Ravi

$$= 660 \times \frac{100}{110} = \text{Rs. } 600$$

Ravi bought the article at the discount of 25%

75% of marked price = Rs. 600

Marked price.

$$= \frac{600 \times 100}{75} = \text{Rs. } 800$$

27. A shopkeeper gains Rs.56 on a toy after allowing 23% discount on its marked price. If his gain is 10%, then the marked price of the toy is:

A. Rs.800

B. Rs.810

C. Rs.740

D. Rs.560

Answer: A

Explanation:

Let marked price of toy be x

$$\text{S.P.} = x \times \frac{77}{100} = \frac{77x}{100}$$

$$\text{C.P.} = x \times \frac{77}{100} \times \frac{100}{110} = \frac{7x}{10}$$

$$\frac{77x}{100} - \frac{7x}{10} = 56$$

$$\frac{7x}{100} = 56$$

$$x = \frac{100 \times 56}{7} = \text{Rs. } 800$$

28. A discount of 2½% is given to the customer on the marked price of an article. A man bought the article for Rs.39. The marked price of the article is:

A. Rs.36.5

B. Rs.42

C. Rs.41.5

D. Rs.40

Answer: D

Explanation:

Suppose printed price = Rs. 100

S.P. = Rs. (100 – 2.5) = Rs. 97.5

$$\text{Marked Price} = \frac{100 \times 39}{97.5} = \text{Rs. } 40$$

29. While selling a watch, a shopkeeper gives a discount of 5%. If he gives a discount of 6%, he earns Rs.15 less as profit. What is the marked price of the watch?

A. Rs.1,400

B. Rs.1,250

C. Rs.750

D. Rs.1,500

Answer:

Explanation:

Let the marked price of watch be x.

$$\frac{x \times 95}{100} - \frac{x \times 94}{100} = 15$$

$$x = 15 \times 100 = \text{Rs. } 1500$$

30. A discount of 16% on the marked price of a book enables a man to buy a pen that costs Rs.80. How much did he pay for the book?

A. Rs.480

B. Rs.500

C. Rs.340

D. Rs.420

Answer: B

Explanation:

Let the amount paid (s.p.) be x

$$16\% \text{ of } x = 80$$

$$x = \frac{80}{16} \times 100$$

$$x = \text{Rs. } 500$$

31. A discount of 24% on the marked price of an article is allowed and then the article is sold for Rs.342. The marked price of the article is.

A. Rs.490

B. Rs.500

C. Rs.430

D. Rs.450

Answer: D

Explanation:

If the marked price of article be x, then.

$$\frac{x \times 76}{100} = 342$$

$$x = \frac{342 \times 100}{76} = \text{Rs. } 450$$

32. The cost price of an article is 64% of the marked price. The gain percentage after allowing a discount of 12% on the marked price is:

A. 48%

B. 37.5%

C. 52%

D. 50.5%

Answer: B

Explanation:

Let marked price of article = Rs. 100

C.P. of article = Rs. 64

S.P. of article = Rs. 88

Profit per cent

$$= \frac{88 - 64}{64} \times 100 = 37.5\%$$

33. An article, which is marked Rs.650, is sold for Rs.572. The discount given is:

A. 13%

B. 12%

C. 26%

D. 21%

Answer: B

Explanation:

Discount = 650 − 572 = Rs. 78

If the discount bex% then

$$\frac{650 \times x}{100} = 78$$

$$x = \frac{78 \times 100}{650} = 12\%$$

34. A shopkeeper sells a badminton racket whose marked price is Rs.30, at a discount of 15% and gives a shuttle cock costing Rs.1.50 free with each racket. Even then he makes a profit of 20%. His cost price, per racket, is:

A. Rs.21.25

B. Rs.21.00

C. Rs.19.75

D. Rs.20.00

Answer: D

Explanation:

Discount = 15%

SP of racket = 85% of Rs. 30 = Rs. 25.50

One shuttle cock of Rs. 1.50 is free.
Actual SP

$$= \text{Rs. } (25.50 - 1.50) = \text{ Rs. } 24$$

He still gains 20%

$$\text{CP} = \frac{100}{120} \times 24 = \text{ Rs. } 20$$

35. A shopkeeper allows 4% discount on his marked price. If the cost price of an article is Rs.100 and he must make a profit of 20%, then his marked price must be:
A. Rs.120
B. Rs.96
C. Rs.130
D. Rs.125

Answer: D
Explanation:
Let the marked price of the article be x
According to the question,

$$96\% \text{ of } x = 120\% \text{ of } 100$$

$$x \times \frac{96}{100} = \frac{100 \times 120}{100}$$

$$x = \frac{100 \times 120}{100} = \text{ Rs. } 125$$

36. A man buys an article for Rs.80 and marks it at Rs.120. He then allows a discount of 40%. What is the loss or gain per cent?
A. 12% loss
B. 12% gain
C. 10% loss
D. 10% gain

Answer: C
Explanation:

$$\text{Discount} = 120 \times \frac{40}{100} = \text{Rs. } 48$$

$$\text{S.P.} = \text{Rs. } (120 - 48) = \text{Rs. } 72$$

$$\text{Loss} = 80 - 72 = \text{Rs. } 8$$

$$\text{Loss } \% = \frac{8}{80} \times 100 = 10\%$$

37. While selling a shirt, a shopkeeper gives a discount of 7%. If he had given a discount of 9%, he would have got Rs.15 less as profit. The marked price of the shirt is:

A. Rs.720

B. Rs.750

C. Rs.600

D. Rs.712.50

Answer: B

Explanation:

Let the marked price of the shirt be x.

Difference of discounts = 2%

2% of x = 15

$$\frac{x \times 2}{100} = 15$$

$$x = \frac{15 \times 100}{2} = \text{Rs. } 750$$

38. A tradesman gives 4% discount on the marked price and gives 1 article free for buying every 15 articles and thus gains 35%. The marked price is increased above the cost price by:

A. 39%

B. 40%

C. 20%

D. 50%

Answer: D

Explanation:

Let the C.P. of each article be Rs. 1

For 15 books, the tradesman gives 1 book free.

C.P. of 15 books = Rs. 16

S.P. of 15 books

$= 16 \times \frac{135}{100} = \text{Rs.} \frac{108}{5}$

S.P. of 1 book

$= \frac{108}{5 \times 15} = \text{Rs.} \frac{36}{25}$

Marked price.

$= \frac{36 \times 100}{25 \times 96} = \frac{3}{2} = \text{Rs. } 1.5$

The required % increase

$= \frac{0.5}{1} \times 100 = 50\%$

39. A fan is listed at Rs.1,500 and a discount of 20% is offered on the list price. What additional discount must be offered to the customer now to bring the net price to Rs.1,104?

A. 10%

B. 8%

C. 12%

D. 15%

Answer: B

Explanation:

First discount = 20%

Price after first discount

$= \text{Rs.} \left(1500 - \frac{20}{100} \times 1500\right)$

$= \text{Rs.} (1500 - 300) = \text{Rs. } 1200$

Let the additional discount be x%

$\left(1200 - \frac{x \times 1200}{100}\right) = 1104$

$1200 - 12x = 1104$

$12x = 1200 - 1104 = 96$

$x = \frac{96}{12} = 8\%$

40. The printed price of an article is Rs.900 but the retailer gets a discount of 40%. He sells the article for Rs.900. Retailer's gain per cent is:

A. 60%

B. 40%

C. $68\frac{1}{3}\%$

D. $66\frac{2}{3}\%$

Answer:

Explanation:

Printed price = Rs. 900

On 40% discount

$$= 900 - \frac{900 \times 40}{100} = 900 - 360$$

C.P. for retailer $= 540$

S.P. $= 900$

Profit $= 900 - 540 = 360$

$$\text{Gain } \% = \frac{360 \times 100}{540}$$

$$= \frac{200}{3} = 66\frac{2}{3}\%$$

41. Gurpreet went to a shop and bought a sofa. She got a 20% discount on it. Had she gotten 25% discount she would have saved Rs. 1000 more. How much did she pay for the sofa?

A. Rs. 5000

B. Rs. 10,000

C. Rs. 20,000

D. Rs. 25000

Answer: C

Explanation:

Let Gurpreet pay Rs. 'A' for the sofa.

We know, she got 20% discount.

Had she gotten 25% discount she would have saved Rs. 1000.

That means 5% extra discount means Rs. 1000

$$\therefore 5\% \text{ of A} = \text{ Rs. } 1000$$

$$\therefore \frac{5}{100} \times A = 1000$$

$$\therefore A = \text{ Rs. } 20000$$

42. Sonali could not decide between a discount of 30% or two successive discounts of 25% and 5%, both given on shopping of Rs. 2000. What is the difference between both the discounts?

A. Rs. 15

B. Rs. 25

C. Rs. 100

D. There is no difference.

Answer: B

Explanation:

30% discount on 200 = 30% of 2000 = Rs. 600

25% discount on 2000 = 25% of 2000 = Rs. 500

Remaining amount = 2000 − 500 = Rs. 1500

Second discount of 5% = 5% of 1500 = Rs. 75

Total discount = 500 + 75 = Rs. 575

So, difference in discounts = Rs. 600 - Rs. 575 = Rs. 25

43. Blackberry announced a discount of 25% on their trousers. Vivek went to shop. He wanted to save Rs. 400 in discount. How many trousers should he buy to do so if each trouser costs Rs. 320?

A. 5

B. 4

C. 10

D. 50

Answer:

Explanation:

Trouser cost = Rs. 320

Discount is 25% of 320 = Rs. 80

For 1 trouser discount is Rs. 80

If Vivek wants to save Rs. 400, so

he needs to buy $\frac{400}{80}$ = 5 trousers

44. Chandrika raised the price of their products by 40%. How much discount should they give to sell the products on no profit no loss basis?

A. 40%

B. 28.5%
C. 22.5%
D. 32.75%

Answer:
Explanation:
Let the initial price be Rs. 100
They increased price by 40%
So, New price = 100 + 40% = 140% of Rs. 100 = Rs. 140
Now to have no profit no loss situation, Chandrika must give Rs. 40 off. How much percent is Rs. 40 of Rs. 140?
Chandrika must give $\frac{40}{140} \times 100 \cong 28.5\%$ discount

45. here is a 10% discount on a dozen pairs of trousers marked at Rs. 8000. How many pair of trousers can be bought with Rs. 2400?
- Published on 03 May 17
A. 7
B. 2
C. 4
D. 8

Answer: C
Explanation:
A dozen pairs means 12 pairs.
Marked price for 12 pairs = Rs. 8000
10% discount, So, Final price = $8000 - 10\%$ of 8000 = Rs. 7200
Price of 1 pair = $7200/12$ = Rs. 600
How many pair of trousers can be bought in Rs. 2400?
Number of pairs of trousers = $\frac{2400}{600}$ = 4 pairs
46. There was 25% off on handbags. Madhu bought a handbag. She also got a 10% discount for paying cash. She paid Rs. 405. What as the price tag on the handbag?
A. Rs. 575
B. Rs. 625
C. Rs. 450
D. Rs. 600

Answer: D

Explanation:

Let the price tag be Rs. A

Initial discount is 25% and cash payment discount is 10%

∴ Equivalent discount will be $\left(25 + 10 - \frac{25\times10}{100}\right) = 32.5\%$

If discount is 32.5%, then Final price = (100 − 32.5)% of Price Tag ∴ 405 = 67.5% of A

$\therefore 405 = \frac{67.5}{100} \times A$

∴ A = Rs. 600 = Price on the price tag

47. Simran gets a discount of 25% on Rs. 3600 ovens. Since she pays cash, she gets additional 2% discount too. How much does she pay?

A. Rs. 2864

B. Rs. 2468

C. Rs. 2548

D. Rs. 2646

Answer: D

Explanation:

25% discount initially, means Price = (100-25) % of 3600= Rs. 2700 2% more discount means 2% of 2700= Rs. 54

Simran pays =2700-54= Rs. 2646

48. George gets a discount of 30% and then 20% on his food bill of Rs. 1250. What is the total discount he got?

A. 44%

B. 55%

C. 52%

D. 25%

Answer: A

Explanation:

$$\text{ADD} = 30 + 20 = 50$$

$$\frac{\text{MULTIPLY}}{100} = \frac{30 \times 20}{100} = 6$$

$\therefore$ Single equivalent $= 50 - 6 = 44\%$

49. When payment is made online, discount offered is 10%. Additional discount of 5% is given to SBI credit card holders. Pratik buys a phone of Rs. 15000 by paying online and pays through his SBI credit card. How much does he need to pay?

A. Rs. 15000

B. Rs. 12825

C. Rs. 13500

D. Rs. 12750

Answer:

Explanation:

Price of phone is Rs. 15000.

Pratik makes online payment, so he gets 10% discount.

So, 10% of 15000 = Rs. 1500

Price becomes = 15000 − 1500 = Rs. 13500

Now since Pratik uses SBI credit card, he gets additional 5% discount.

So 5% of Rs. 13500 = $\frac{5}{100} \times 13500$ = Rs. 675

So, Final bill will be Rs. 13500 - Rs. 675 = Rs. 12825

50. How much does the sarees sales revenue of Uday increase, if Uday announces 25% discount on sarees and the saree sales volume increase by 40%?

A. 15% increase

B. 5% increase

C. -5% increase

D. There is no increase.

Answer: B

Explanation:

In such cases take a simple example.

Let Uday sell 10 sarees for Rs. 100 each.

So his revenue = 10×100 = Rs. 1000

Now he gives 25% discount.

So, price of each saree = $(100 - 25)\%$ of 100 = Rs. 75

Sales volume increases by 40%

So now Uday sells 140% of 10 = 14 sarees.

New revenue of Uday = 14×75 = Rs. 1050

Increase in revenue = $1050 - 1000$ = Rs. 50

Percent increase = $\frac{50}{1000} \times 100 = 5\%$

51. After deducting a commission of 5%, a TV set costs Rs. 9595. Its marked price is

A. Rs. 10000

B. Rs. 10074.75

C. Rs. 10100

D. Rs. 12000

Answer:

Explanation:

So 5% commission will be charged on Rs. 9595.

So the commission will be 5% of 9595 = $\frac{5}{100} \times 9595$ = Rs. 479.75

Marked price = Selling Price + Commission = $9595 + 479.75$

∴ Marked price = Rs. 10074.75

52. A vase has a marked price of Rs. 560. Simran pays Rs. 336 for it because she got 2 successive discounts, one of 20% and other of _____.

A. 20

B. 15%

C. 25%

D. 10%

Answer:

Explanation:

Total Discount = Rs. 560 -Rs. 336 = Rs. 224

Rs. 224 is how much percent of Rs. 560?

It is $\frac{224}{560} \times 100 = 40\%$

Let second discount be ' A%

ADD = 20 + A

$$\frac{\text{MULTIPLY}}{100} = \frac{20A}{100}$$

$$\therefore \text{ Single equivalent } = 40 = 20 + A - \frac{20A}{100}$$

$\therefore A = 25\%$

53. Raj decides to sell his watch at 5% discount. But his brother buys it from him, and he gives his brother 8% discount. Due to this Raj gets Rs. 45 less in the profit. What was the marked price of the watch?

A. Rs. 1500

B. Rs. 1800

C. Rs. 9000

D. Rs. 6000

Answer: A

Explanation:

Difference in discount = 8% − 5% = 3%

Due to this 3% Raj gets Rs. 45 less

That means 3% of Marked Price = 45

$$\therefore \frac{3}{100} \times MP = 45$$

$\therefore MP =$ Rs. 1500

54. 30% discount on Rs. 1000 and 2 successive discounts of 15% and 15% will have a difference of

A. Rs. 22.5

B. Rs. 10

C. Rs. 150

D. Rs. 0

Answer: A

Explanation:

30% discount = 30% of 1000 = Rs. 300

Now, if you offer two successive discounts of 15% each, it works out to First discount of 15% = 15% of 1000 = Rs. 150

After discount value = Rs. 1000 - Rs. 150 = Rs. 850

Second discount of 15% = 15% of Rs. 850 = $\frac{15}{100} \times 850$ = Rs. 127.5

Difference = 300 – (150 + 127.5) = Rs. 22.5

55. 2 successive discounts with the first being 20%, were given on a table having marked price of Rs. 6400. Finally it was sold for Rs. 4608. How much was the 2nd discount?

A. 20%

B. 10%

C. 5%

D. 25%

Answer: B

Explanation:

Price after 1 "t discount of 20% = (100 – 20)% = 80% of Marked Price ∴ Price = $\frac{80}{100} \times 6400$ = Rs. 5120

SP = (100-Discount)% of Price

∴ $4608 = (100\text{-Discount})\% \times 5120$

∴ $\frac{(100\text{-Discount})}{100} = \frac{4608}{5120}$ → Converting discount percent to normal fraction

∴ Discount = 10% = This much per cent is the 2nd discount.

56. Marked price of a TV is 20% more than its cost price. Yet Ajay gives a discount of 30% while selling the TV. How much per cent loss did he incur?

A. 10%

B. 16%

C. 5%

D. 50%

Answer: B

Explanation:

Let CP = Rs. 100

Marked Price = 20% more than CP

∴ MP = Rs. 120

Discount = 30% on marked price

$\therefore$ SP = (100 – 30)% of MP

$$\therefore SP = \frac{70}{100} \times 120 = \text{Rs. } 84$$

$$\text{Loss }\% = \frac{100 - 84}{100} \times 100 = 16\%$$

57. In order that there may be a profit of 20% after allowing a discount of 40% on the marked price, the cost price of an article must be increased by?

A. 66.67%

B. 33.33%

C. 50%

D. 100%

Answer: D

Explanation:

Discount = 40%

SP = (100 – 40)% of MP = 60% of MP

Profit = 20%

$\therefore$ SP = (100 + 20)% of CP

$\therefore$ 60% × MP = 120% of CP

$$\therefore CP = \frac{1}{2} MP$$

$\therefore$ MP = 2CP

Since, MP is twice of CP, we need to increase CP by 100% to make it MP.

58. If successive discounts are 10%, 20% and 30%, then what is its single equivalent discount?

A. 60%

B. 40.56%

C. 49.6%

D. 30%

Answer:

Explanation:

Take Value = 100

For 1st discount of 10%, 1 st value = (100 – 10)% of 100 = 90% of 100 = 90

For 2nd discount of 20%, 2nd value = (100 – 20)% of 90 = 80% of 90 = 72

For 3rd discount of 30%, Final value = $(100 - 30)\%$ of 72 = $\frac{70}{100} \times 72 = 50.4$

So, Discount = 100 - Final value = $100 - 50.4 = 49.6\%$

59. If a book costs Rs. 900 and is sold with a profit of 10% and discount of 12% then, the advertised price is?

A. Rs. 1050

B. Rs. 1125

C. Rs. 812.5

D. Rs. 1225

Answer: B

Explanation:

Since profit of 10% is there, $\therefore SP = (100 + 10)\%$ of CP

$= \frac{110}{100} \times 900 =$ Rs. 990

Discount = 12%

So, $SP = (100 - 12)\%$ of List Price

$\therefore 990 = \frac{88}{100} \times LP$

$\therefore LP =$ Rs. 1125

60. During monsoon clearance sale, Amit buys a shirt at double discount of 20% and 10%. At what price he bought the shirt if marked price was Rs. 1000?

A. Rs. 720

B. Rs. 800

C. Rs. 700

D. Rs. 850

Answer: A

Explanation:

1st discount is 20%

So price after discount = $100 - 20$

= 80% of marked price = 80% of 1000 = Rs. 800

2nd discount = 10%

So price after 2nd discount = $100 - 10\%$

= 90% of new price = 90% of 800 = Rs. 720

Introduction

The circle is a familiar shape, and it has a host of geometric properties that can be proved using the traditional Euclidean format. But it is sometimes useful to work in co-ordinates and this requires us to know the standard equation of a circle, how to interpret that equation and how to find the equation of a tangent to a circle. This video will explore these facets of a circle, using co-ordinate geometry.

- In geometry, Circle is an important shape for the students in Mathematics. The application of the Circle in many parts of science such as Mathematics, Physics and Astronomy is based on the theoretical importance of the circle.

- Circle is a curved line that has an equal interval from the focal point and is connected to the starting point.

- On the other hand, Circle is a locus of every point that has the same distance from the center. It is a unique type of ellipse in that its foci are coincident and its eccentricity constant.

- The radius of the circle is a curved line from the origin to the outer side of the circle. The diameter of the circle is a curved line that divides the whole circle into two same sectors and the length of the diameter is always twice its radius.

Definition Of Circle

A circle is a closed two-dimensional figure in which the set of all the points in the plane is equidistant from a given point called "centre". Every line that passes through the circle forms the line of reflection symmetry. Also, it has rotational symmetry around the centre for every angle. The circle formula in the plane is given as:

$(x-h)^2 + (y-k)^2 = r^2$

where (x,y) are the coordinate points (h,k) is the coordinate of the centre of a circle and r is the radius of a circle.

Circle Shaped Objects

There are many objects we have seen in the real world that are circular in shape. Some of the examples are:

- Ring
- CD/Disc
- Bangles
- Coins
- Wheels
- Button
- Dartboard
- Hula hoop

We can observe many such examples in our day-to-day life.

How to Draw a Circle

In math's projects for class 10 on circles, the construction of a circle, all the properties and terminologies are explained in detail. To understand what circles are in simple terms, go through circles for class 10, and also try the following exercise –

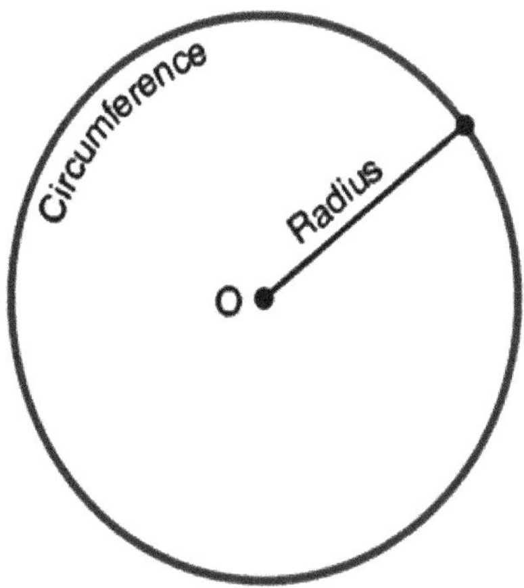

1. Take an empty sheet of paper and mark a single point on the sheet, somewhere in the middle of the sheet, and name it to point O.
2. Select a random length for radius, for example, 3 cm.
3. Using a ruler, keep the reference zero mark on point O and randomly mark 3 cm away from point O in all directions.
4. Mark as many points as you want away from point O, but all of them should be exactly 3 cm away from point O.

Parts of Circle

A circle has different parts based on the positions and their properties. The different parts of a circle are explained below in detail.

- **Annulus-**The region bounded by two concentric circles. It is basically a ring-shaped object. See the figure below.

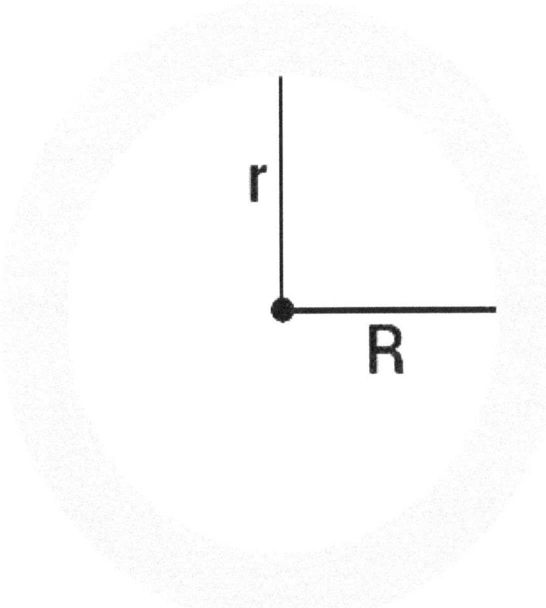

Annulus

- Arc – It is basically the connected curve of a circle.
- Sector – A region bounded by two radii and an arc.
- Segment- A region bounded by a chord and an arc lying between the chord's endpoints. It is to be noted that segments do not contain the centre.

See the figure below explaining the arc, sector and segment of a circle.

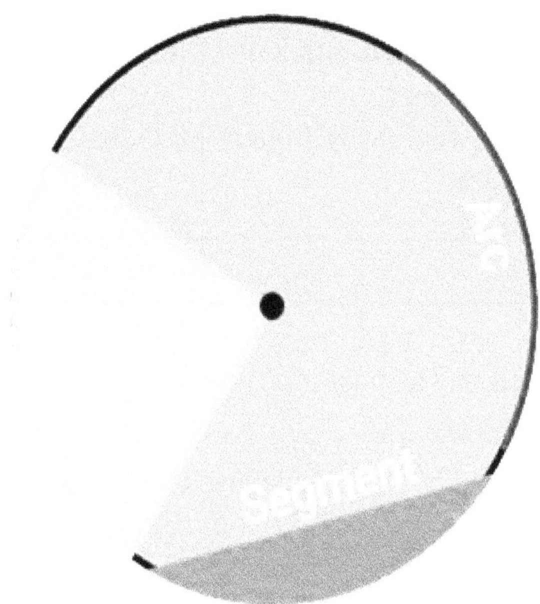

- **Centre –** It is the midpoint of a circle.
- **Chord-** A line segment whose endpoints lie on the circle.
- **Diameter-** A line segment having both the endpoints on the circle and is the largest chord of the circle.
- **Radius-** A line segment connecting the centre of a circle to any point on the circle itself.
- **Secant-** A straight line cutting the circle at two points. It is also called an extended chord.
- **Tangent-** A coplanar straight line touching the circle at a single point.

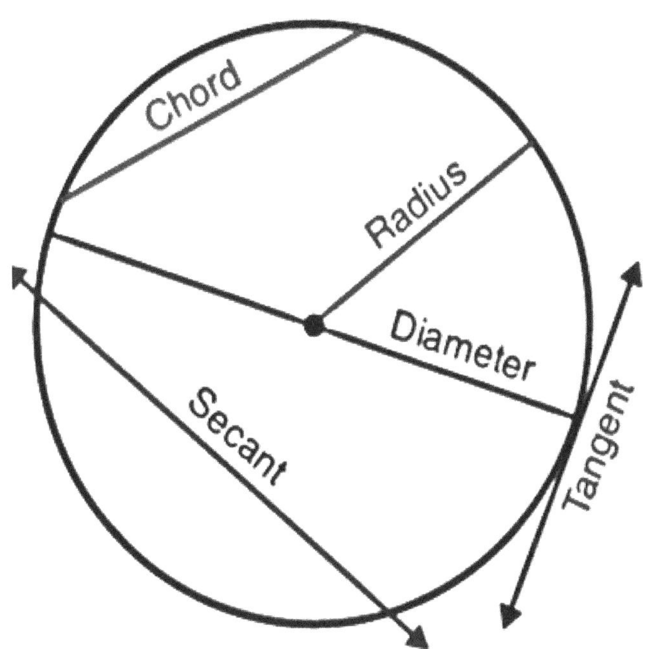

Radius of Circle (r)

A line segment connecting the centre of a circle to any point on the circle itself". The radius of the circle is denoted by "R" or "r".

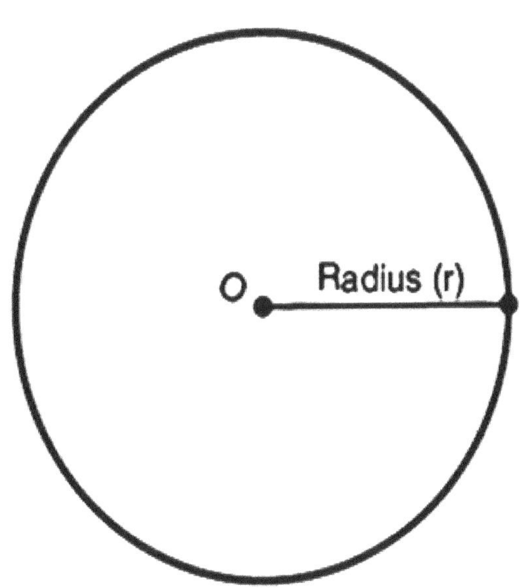

Diameter (d) of Circle

A line segment having both the endpoints on the circle. It is twice the length of radius i.e., **d = 2r**. From the diameter, the radius of the circle formula is obtained as r= d/2.

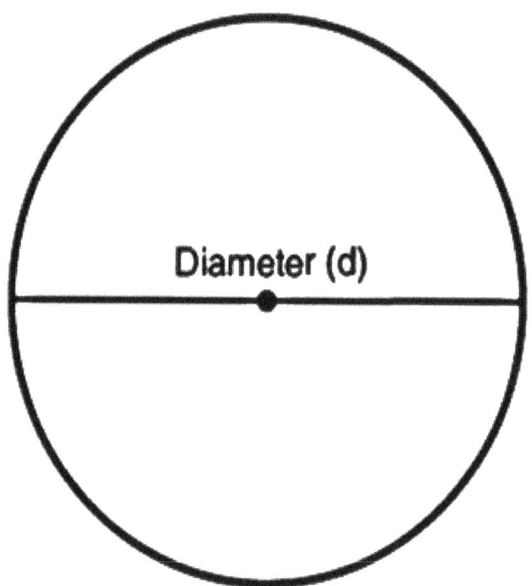

Circle Formulas

We know that a circle is a two-dimensional curve-shaped figure, and the two different parameters used to measure the circle are:

- Area of circle
- Circumference of a circle

Area and Circumference of a Circle

Circumference (C)	The circumference of a circle is defined as the distance around the circle. The word 'perimeter' is also sometimes used, although this usually refers to the distance around polygons, figures made up of the straight-line segment.	

	A circle circumference formula is given by $\mathbf{C = \pi d = 2\ \pi\ r}$ Where, $\pi = 3.1415$	
Area (A)	The area of a circle is the amount of space occupied by the circle. The circle formula to find the area is given by. **Area of a circle =** $\boldsymbol{\pi r^2}$	

Circle Area Proof

We know that Area is the space occupied by the circle.

Consider a concentric circle having an external circle radius to be ‘r.’

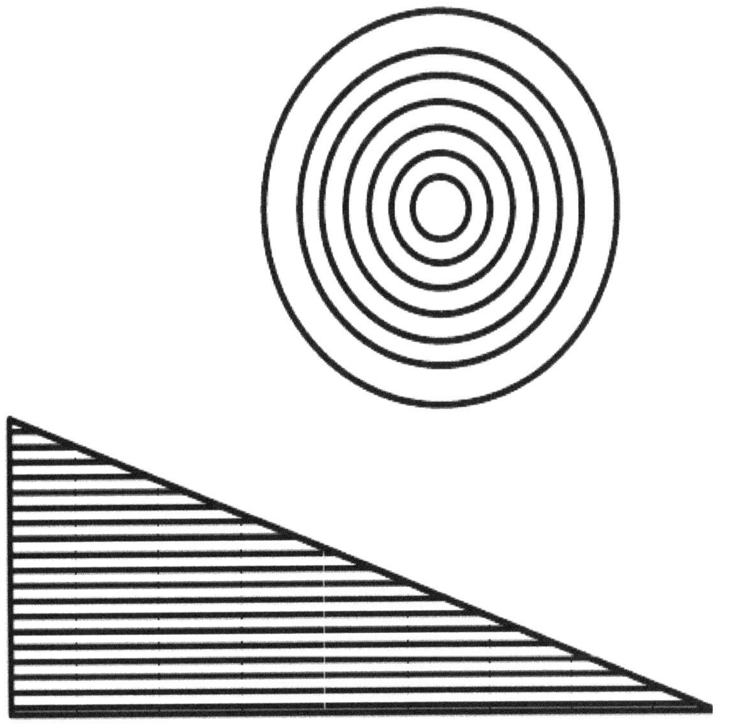

pen all the concentric circles to form a right-angled triangle.

The outer circle would form a line having length $2\pi r$ forming the base.

The height would be 'r'

Therefore, the area of the right-angled triangle formed would be equal to the area of a circle.

Area of a circle = Area of triangle = (1/2) ×b ×h

= (1/2) × 2π r × r

Therefore, Area of a circle = πr2

Properties of Circles

The important basic properties of circles are as follows:

- The outer line of a circle is at equidistant from the centre.
- The diameter of the circle divides it into two equal parts.
- Circles which have equal radii are congruent to each other.
- Circles which are different in size or having different radii are similar.
- The diameter of the circle is the largest chord and is double the radius.

Radius Of a Circle and Chord

The radius of a circle is the distance from the center of the circle to any point on it's circumference. It is usually denoted by 'R' or 'r'.
The area and circumference of a circle are also measured in terms of radius.
Circumference of circle = 2π (Radius)
Area of circle = π $(\text{Radius})^2$

Definition

A radius is a measure of distance from the center of any circular object to its outermost edge or boundary. A radius is not only a dimension of a circle but also for a sphere, semi-sphere, a cone with a circular base, a cylinder having circular bases.

A circle can be defined as the locus of a point moving in a plane, in such a manner that its distance from a fixed point is always constant. The fixed point is known as the center of the circle and distance between any point on the circle and its center is called the radius of a circle.

Diameter of a Circle

The diameter of a circle is the length of the line starting from one point on a circle to another point and passing through the center of the circle. It is equal to twice the radius of the circle. It is usually denoted by 'd' or 'D'.

Diameter = 2 x Radius

Or

Radius = Diameter/2

Diameter is the longest chord of the circle.

Also, we can express the area and circumference of a circle with respect to the diameter.

Circumference of circle = π (Diameter)

Area of circle = $\pi/4$ (Diameter)^2

Radius, Diameter and Chord

We have already discussed radius and diameter of circle. Now suppose, there is a line and a Circle given on a plane. The line could touch a circle at one point or intersect at two points or it could be non-intersecting.

Explanation:

Given a line and a Circle, it could either be touching the circle, interesting line or non-touching.

Consider any line AB and a circle. Then according to the relative positions of the line and the circle, three possibilities can arise as shown in the given figure.

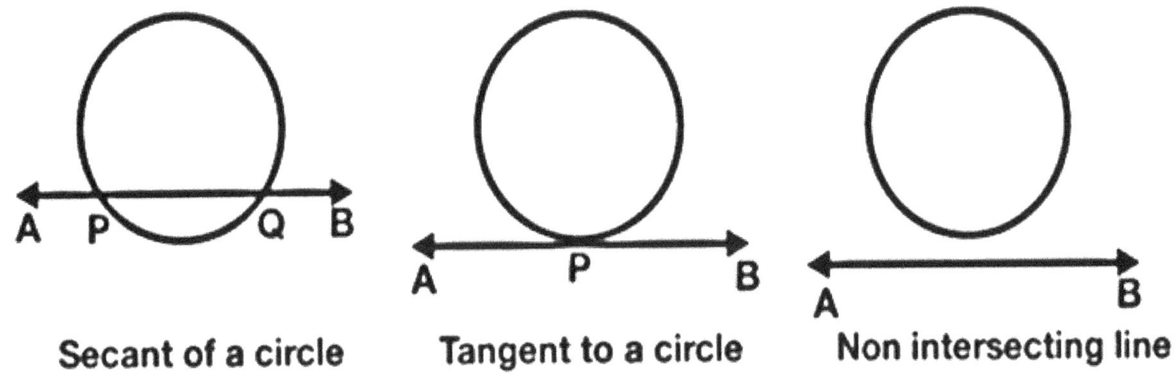

Line AB intersects the given circle at two distinct points P and Q. The line AB in this case is referred to as secant of the circle. Points P and Q lie on the circumference of the circle, but they do not pass through the center of the circle 'O', hence line segment PQ is known as a chord of the circle as its endpoints lie on the circle.

Therefore, the chord of a circle can be defined as a line segment joining any two distinct points on the circle's circumference. A chord passing through the center of a circle is known as the diameter of the circle and it is the largest chord of the circle. This diameter is twice that of the radius of a circle i.e., D=2r, where 'D' is the diameter and 'r' is the radius.

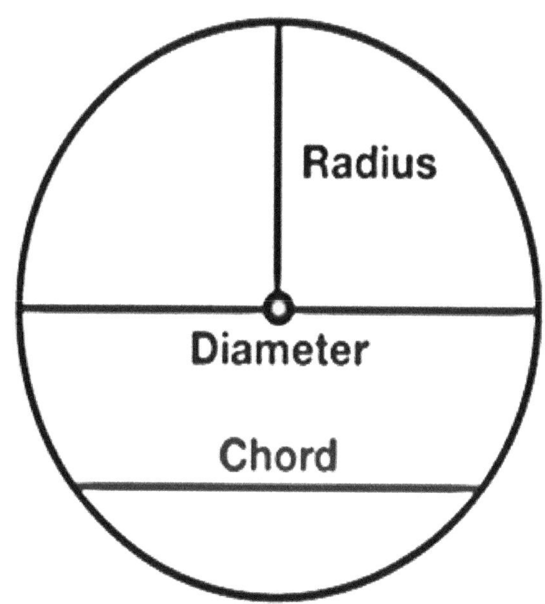

Radius of a circle = Diameter/2
Or

Diameter of a circle = 2 × Radius

Equation

The equation of a circle includes the radius, and it is given by:

$(x-h)^2 + (y-k)^2 = r^2$

Where (h, k) is the center of circle.

Radius of circle from Area

Since, the formula for area of a circle is given by:

Area of circle = $\pi(\text{Radius})^2$

Therefore,

Radius2 = Area/π

Radius = √(Area/π)

How to find Radius with Circumference?

If we know the circumference of the circle, then we can easily find its radius. Let us understand by example.

Suppose the circumference is 40cms, then find the radius.

Since, Circumference, $C = 2\pi r$

$R = C/2\pi$

$R = 40/2\pi$

$R = 6.37$ cm

Radius Formula

With respect to area and circumference, we can write the formula for the radius as:

- $R = C/2\pi$ And $R = \sqrt{(A/\pi)}$
- Also, $R = D/2$

Chord of a Circle Theorems

Theorem 1: The perpendicular line drawn from the center of a circle to a chord bisects the chord.

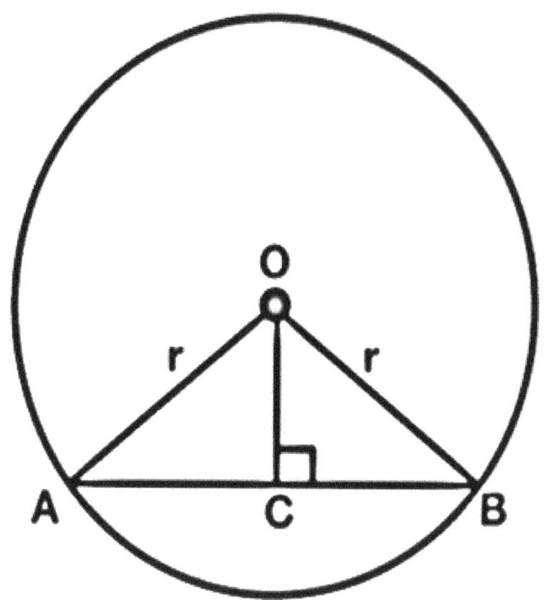

Given: AB= Chord; OC⊥AB

To prove: AC=BC

Construction: Draw OA and OB

Proof:

S. No.	Statement	Reason
In ΔOAC and ΔOBC		
1	OA = OB	Radii of the same circle
2	OC = OC	Common
3	∠OCA = ∠OCB	Each angle measure 90 degrees
4	ΔOAC ≅ ΔOBC	By RHS congruence criterion
5	AC = CB	By CPCT (Corresponding parts of congruent triangles)

The converse of the above theorem is also true.

Theorem 2: The line drawn through the centre of the circle to bisect a chord is perpendicular to the chord.

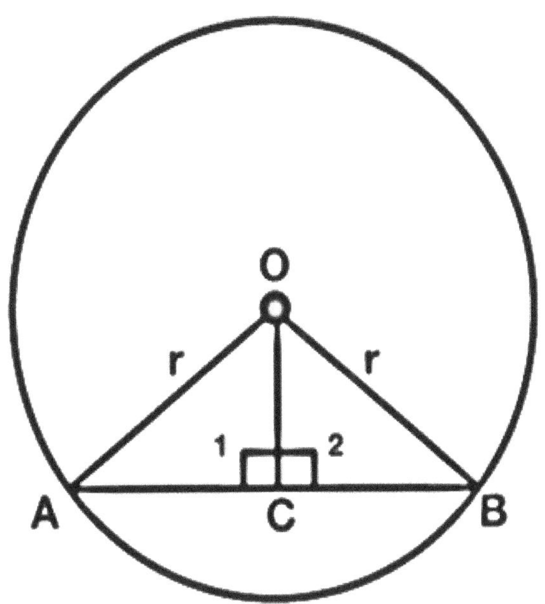

Given: C is the midpoint of the chord AB of the circle with centre of circle at O

To prove: OC⊥AB

Construction: Join OA, OB and OC

Proof:

S.No.	Statement	Reason
In ΔOAC and ΔOBC		
1	OA = OB	Radii of the same circle
2	OC = OC	Common side
3	AC = BC	Given
4	ΔOAC ≅ ΔOBC	By SSS congruency
5	∠1 = ∠2	Corresponding parts of congruent triangle
6	∠1 + ∠2 = 180°	Linear pair angles
7	∠1 = ∠2 = 90°	From statements 5 and 6
8	OC ⊥ AB	From statement 7

Secant of a Circle

To learn about the Secant of a circle, let's recall what a circle is. A circle is a closed loop. In a circle, every point on the circle is at an equal distance from the centre O. In a secant, the line intersects the circle at two points. But a tangent intersects the circle at only one point around its outer line. This is the basic difference between a secant and a tangent. But the common fact between them is both the lines are drawn from outside of the circle. Let us learn more here.

Secant of the Circle Definition

A straight line that intersects a circle in two points is called a secant line. A chord is the line segment that joins two distinct points of the circle. A chord is in a unique secant line and every secant line defines a unique chord. In geometry, a secant is a line that cuts any curve in at least two different points. Secant means 'to cut' extracted from a Latin word 'secare'. While in a circle, a secant will touch the circle in exactly two points and a chord is the line segment defined by these two points, that is the interval on a secant whose endpoints are these two points.

Secant of a Circle Formula

If a secant and a tangent of a circle are drawn from a point outside the circle, then.
Lengths of the secant × its external segment = (length of the tangent segment)^2

Diameter of Circle – Secant

A secant is an extension of a chord in a circle which is a straight-line segment of which the endpoints lie on the circle. If the same chord passes through the centre of the circle, then it is a diameter. So, an extended Diameter is a secant.

Intersecting Secants

When two secants of a circle intersect each other at a point outside the circle, there becomes an intersecting relationship between those two-line segments.

If PQ and RS are the intersecting secants of the given circle then $(P + Q). Q = (R + S) .S$

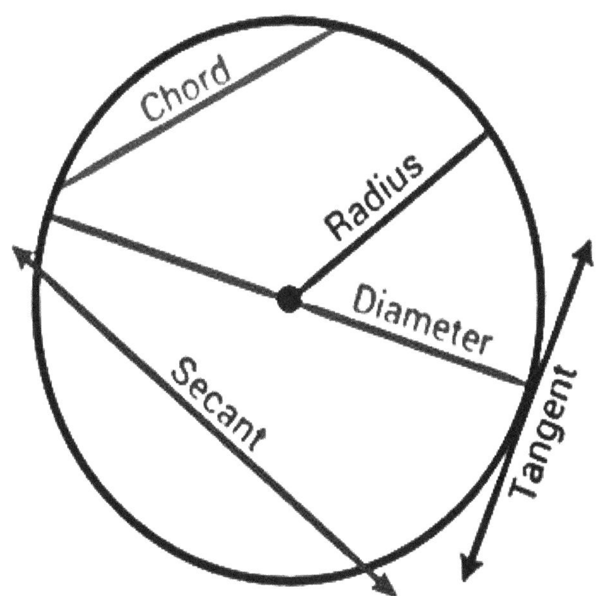

In the above figure, you can see:

- Blue line segment is the secant
- Red shows the tangent
- Green is the chord of circle

How do you find the secant of a circle?

A part of a line between the two endpoints is called a line segment.

Secant	**Chord**
It intersects the circle at two points	It touches the circle at two points
It is drawn from outside the circle	It lies within the circle

Sector Of a Circle

A circle has always been an important shape among all geometrical figures. There are various concepts and formulas related to a circle. The sectors and segments are perhaps the most useful of them. In this article, we shall focus on the concept of a sector of a circle along with area and perimeter of a sector.

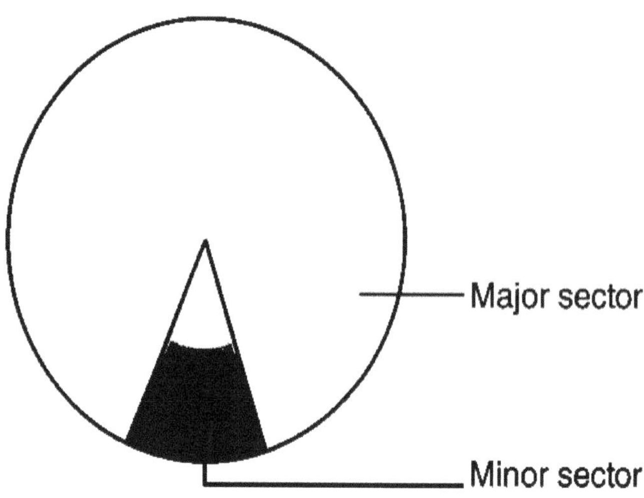

A sector is said to be a part of a circle made of the arc of the circle along with its two radii. It is a portion of the circle formed by a portion of the circumference (arc) and radii of the circle at both endpoints of the arc. The shape of a sector of a circle can be compared with a slice of pizza or a pie.

Before we start learning more about the sector, first let us learn some basics of the circle.

What is a Circle?

A circle is a locus of points equidistant from a given point located at the centre of the circle. The common distance from the centre of the circle to its point is called the radius. Thus, the circle is defined by its centre (o) and radius (r). A circle is also defined by two of its properties, such as area and perimeter. The formulas for both the measures of the circle are given by.

- **Area of a circle = πr^2**
- **The perimeter of a circle = $2\pi r$**

What is Sector of a circle?

The sector is basically a portion of a circle which could be defined based on these three points mentioned below:

- A circular sector is the portion of a disk enclosed by two radii and an arc.
- A sector divides the circle into two regions, namely Major and Minor Sector.
- The smaller area is known as the Minor Sector, whereas the region having a greater area is known as Major Sector.

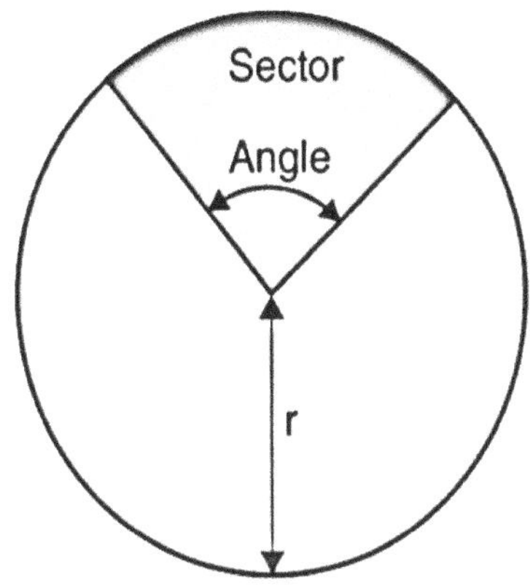

Area of a sector

In a circle with radius r and centre at O, let $\angle POQ = \theta$ (in degrees) be the angle of the sector. Then, the area of a sector of circle formula is calculated using the unitary method.

For the given angle the area of a sector is represented by:

The angle of the sector is 360°, area of the sector, i.e., the Whole circle = πr^2

When the Angle is 1°, area of sector = $\pi r^2/360°$

So, when the angle is θ, area of sector, OPAQ, is defined as.

$$A = (\theta/360°) \times \pi r^2$$

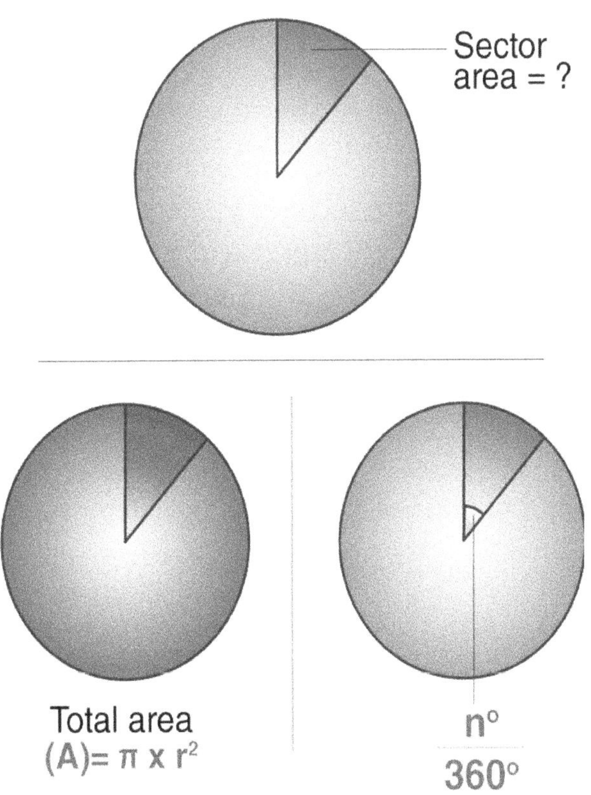

Let the angle be 45 °. Therefore, the circle will be divided into 8 parts, as per the given in the below figure.

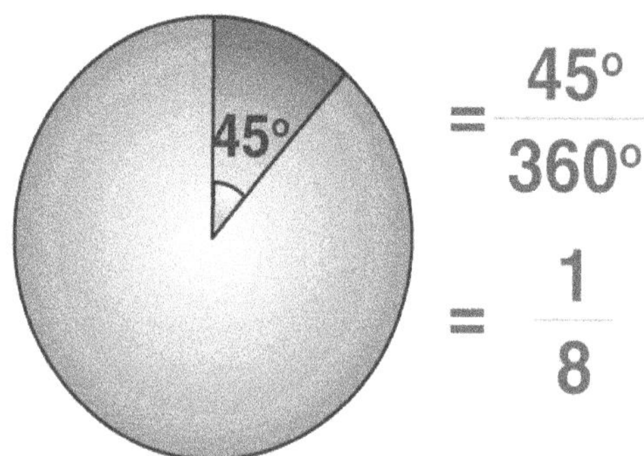

Now the area of the sector for the above figure can be calculated as **(1/8) (3.14×r×r).**

Thus, the Area of a sector is calculated as:

$$\mathbf{A = (\theta/360) \times 22/7 \times r^2}$$

Length of the Arc of Sector Formula

Similarly, the length of the arc (PQ) of the sector with angle θ, is given by.

$$\mathbf{l = (\theta/360) \times 2\pi r \text{ (or) } l = (\theta\pi r)/180}$$

Area of Sector with respect to Length of the Arc

If the length of the arc of the sector is given instead of the angle of the sector, there is a different way to calculate the area of the sector. Let the length of the arc be *l*. For the radius of a circle equal to r units, an arc of length r units will subtend 1 radian at the centre. Hence, it can be concluded that an arc of length l will subtend l/r, the angle at the centre. So, if l is the length of the arc, r is the radius of the circle and θ is the angle subtended at the centre, then.

$\theta = l/r$, where θ is in radians.

When the angle of the sector is 2π, then the area of the sector (whole sector) is πr^2.

When the angle is 1, the area of the sector $= \pi r^2/2\pi = r^2/2$

So, when the angle is θ, area of the sector $= \theta \times r^2/2$

$A = (l/r) \times (r^2/2)$

$$\mathbf{A = (lr)/2}$$

Perimeter of a Sector

The perimeter of the sector of a circle is the length of two radii along with the arc that makes the sector. In the following diagram, a sector is shown in yellow colour.

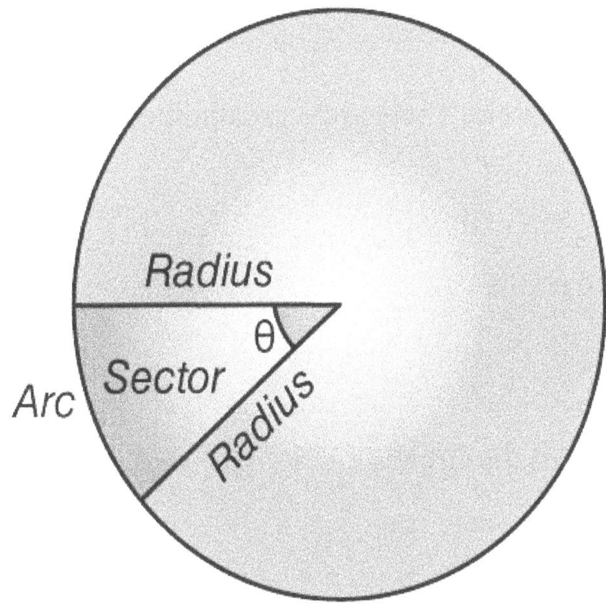

The perimeter should be calculated by doubling the radius and then adding it to the length of the arc.

Perimeter of a Sector Formula

The formula for the perimeter of the sector of a circle is given below:

Perimeter of sector = radius + radius + arc length

Perimeter of sector = 2 radius + arc length

Arc length is calculated using the relation:

Arc length = l = (θ/360) × 2πr

Therefore,

Perimeter of a Sector = 2 Radius + (θ/360) × 2πr)

Tangent of a Circle

Before understanding the concept of the tangent of a circle, let us understand about the circle and how the line intersects the circle in this article.

What is the Tangent of a Circle

A tangent to a circle is a line which intersects the circle at only one point. The common point between the tangent and the circle is called the point of contact.

Given, a line to a circle could either be intersecting, non-intersecting or just touching the circle or non-touching.

Consider any line AB and a circle. There are 3 possibilities as shown in the below:

(1) Line

AB
intersects the circle at two points.
P
and
Q
Such a line is called *secant* of the circle.
P
and
Q
are the points on the circle.
PQ
is a chord of the circle.

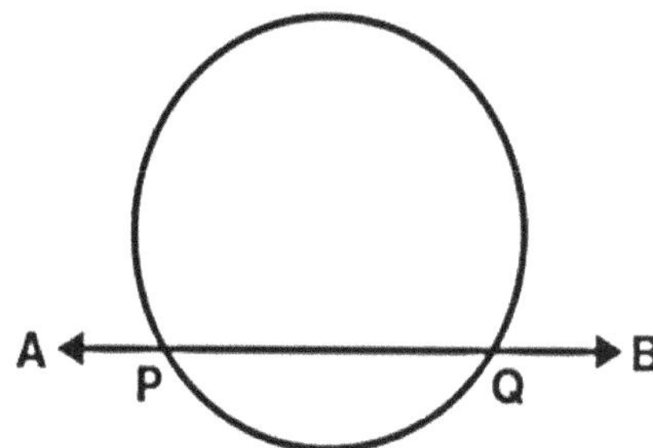

(2) Line

AB
touches the circle exactly at one point,
P
Such a line is called the *tangent* to the circle.

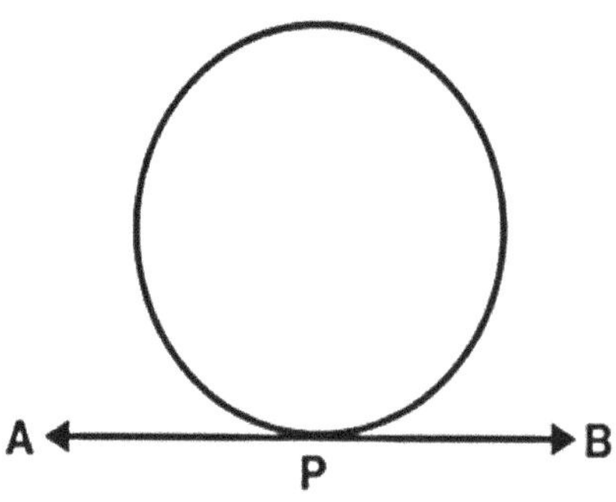

(3) Line

AB
does not touch the circle at any point and is referred to as a non-intersecting line.

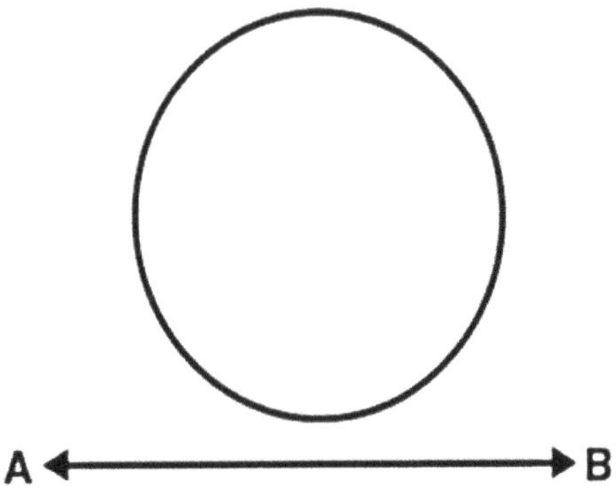

Tangent of a Circle Example

Imagine a bicycle moving on a road. If we look at its wheel, we observe that it touches the road at just one point. The road can be considered as a tangent to the wheel.

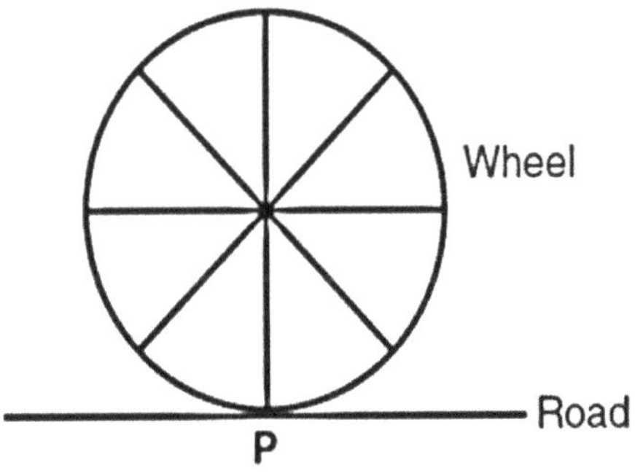

Tangent to a circle

It is to be noted that there can be one and only one tangent through any given point on the circle.

Concentric Circles Meaning

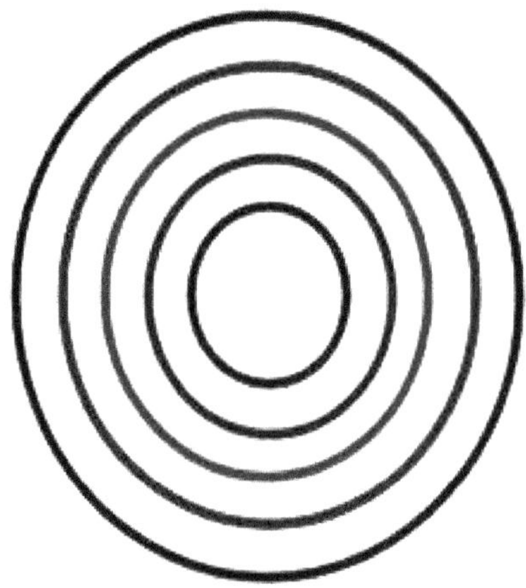

The circles with a common centre are known as concentric circles and have different radii. In other words, it is defined as two or more circles that have the same centre point. The region between two concentric circles is of different radii is known as an annulus.

Concentric Circle Equations

Let the equation of the circle with centre (-g, -f) and radius $\sqrt{[g^2+f^2-c]}$ be.

$x^2 + y^2 + 2gx + 2fy + c = 0$

Therefore, the equation of the circle concentric with the other circle be.

$x^2 + y^2 + 2gx + 2fy + c' = 0$

It is observed that both the equations have the same centre (-g, -f), but they have different radii, where $c \neq c'$.

Similarly, a circle with centre (h, k), and the radius is equal to r, then the equation becomes.

$(x - h)^2 + (y - k)^2 = r^2$

Therefore, the equation of a circle concentric with the circle is

$\mathbf{(x - h)^2 + (y - k)^2 = r_1^2}$

Where $r \neq r_1$

By assigning different values to the radius in the above equation, we shall get a family of circles.

Concentric Circles – Theorem

In two concentric circles, the chord of the larger circle, which touches the smaller circle, is bisected at the point of contact.

Proof

Given:

Consider two concentric circles C_1 and C_2, with centre O and a chord AB of the larger circle C_1, touching the smaller circle C_2 at the point P as shown in the figure below.

Construction:

Join OP.

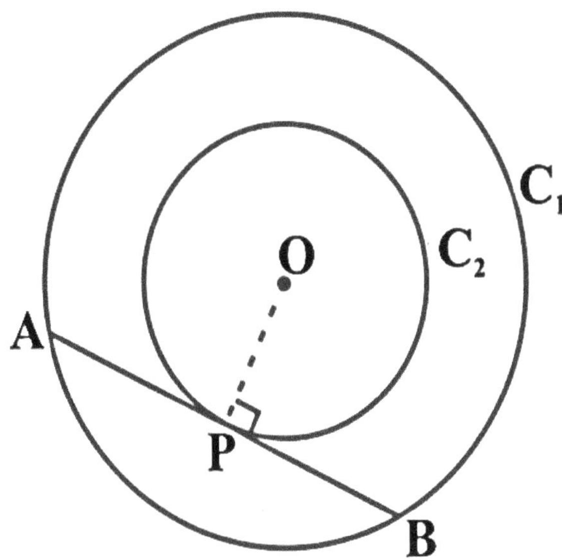

To prove: AP = BP

Proof:

Since AB is the chord of larger circle C_1, it becomes the tangent to C_2 at P.

OP is the radius of circle C_2.

We know that the radius is perpendicular to the tangent at the point of contact.

So, $OP \perp AB$

Now AB is a chord of the circle C1 and $OP \perp AB$.

Therefore, OP is the bisector of the chord AB.

Thus, the perpendicular from the centre bisects the chord, i.e., AP = BP.

Region Between Concentric Circles

As mentioned above, the region between two concentric circles is called the annulus. However, we can find the perimeter and area of the annulus using appropriate formulas.

The area of the annulus is calculated by subtracting the area of smaller circles from the area of the larger circle.

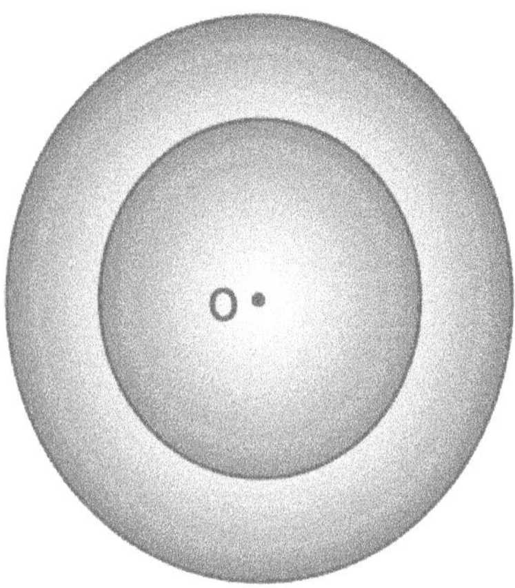

Suppose R is the radius of the larger circle and r is the radius of the smaller circle such that the area of the region bounded by these two circles is given by:

Area of annulus = $\pi R^2 - \pi r^2$

Learn more about annulus here.

The Formula of the Circles

- A circle has a specific shape, and it is denoted by the group of points that lie on a plane that are equidistant from the origin of the circle. The formulas of the circle are mainly generated to determine the diameter, area and perimeter of the circle.

- The below image shows that the AB is a straight line divided by the circle into two equal parts with the radius r and circumference C.

- Formulas for calculating the diameter, area and circumference of the circle is $P=2\times a$, where P is the diameter of any circle and 'a' is the radius of that circle.

- To determine the area of the circle is $D= \pi\times$ a2, where is the radius, D is the area of the circle and $\pi = 22/7$. The formula of the circumference of the circle is $A=2\times\pi\times r$. Where A denotes the circumference and r is the radius of the circle.

Properties of the Circle

- The circle word is taken from the Greek word "Kirkus" which means the hoop or ring. There are several types of properties of the circle in mathematics and its connection with polygons, straight lines and angles shows the various importance's in mathematics.

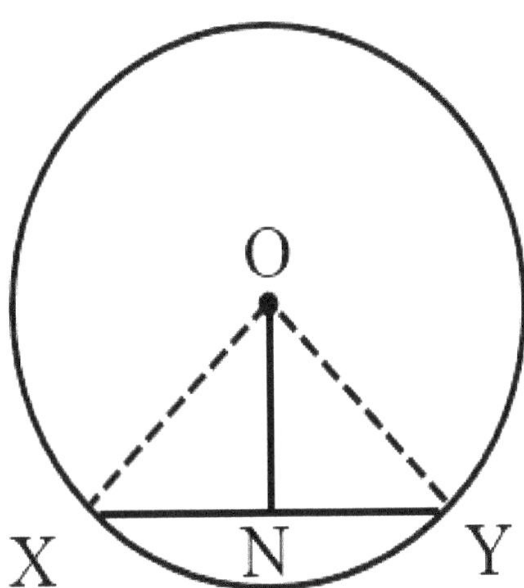

- Consider a circle with radius O and XY is the chord of that circle; it means ON is perpendicular to XY.
- To determine the properties of a circle towards the chord is to prove XN=YN. Let, in the triangle, XON and triangle YON have the radius XO=OY and the sides ON are common sides for both triangles.
- Therefore, angle XON and angle YON is a right angle that is a 90-degree angle. Again, the triangle XON≃ triangle YON [from the R.H.S congruence rule] and therefore, XN=YN [from CPCT theorem].

MULTIPLE CHOICE QUESTIONS

1. A circle has a number of tangents equal to

A. 0

B. 1

C. 2

D. Infinite

Answer: D

Explanation:

A circle has infinitely many tangents, touching the circle at infinite points on its circumference.

2. A tangent intersects the circle at:

A. One point

B. Two distinct point

C. At the circle

D. None of the above

Answer: A

Explanation:

A tangent touch the circle only on its boundary and do not cross through it.

3. A circle can have ______parallel tangents at a single time.

A. One

B. Two

C. Three

D. Four

Answer: B

Explanation:

A circle can have two parallel tangents at the most.

4. If the angle between two radii of a circle is 110°, then the angle between the tangents at the ends of the radii is:

A. 90°

B. 50°
C. 70°
D. 40°

Answer: C
Explanation:
If the angle between two radii of a circle is 110°, then the angle between tangents is 180° – 110° = 70°. (By circles and tangents properties)

5. The length of the tangent from an external point A on a circle with centre O is
A. always greater than OA
B. equal to OA
C. always less than OA
D. cannot be estimated

Answer: C
Explanation:
Since the tangent is perpendicular to the radius of the circle, then the angle between them is 90°. Thus, OA is the hypotenuse for the right triangle OAB, which is right-angled at B. As we know, for any right triangle, the hypotenuse is the longest side. Therefore the length of the tangent from an external point is always less than the OA.

6. AB is a chord of the circle and AOC is its diameter such that angle ACB = 50°. If AT is the tangent to the circle at the point A, then BAT is equal to
A. 65°
B. 60°
C. 50°
D. 40°

Answer: C
Explanation:
As per the given question:

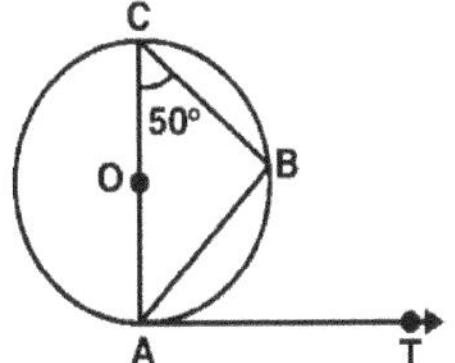

$\angle ABC = 90°$ (angle in Semicircle is right angle)

In ΔACB

$\angle A + \angle B + \angle C = 180°$

$\angle A = 180° - (90° + 50°)$

$\angle A = 40°$

Or $\angle OAB = 40°$

Therefore, $\angle BAT = 90° - 40° = 50°$

7. If TP and TQ are the two tangents to a circle with centre O so that $\angle POQ = 110°$, then $\angle PTQ$ is equal to

A. 60°

B. 70°

C. 80°

D. 90°

Answer: B

Explanation:

As per the given question:

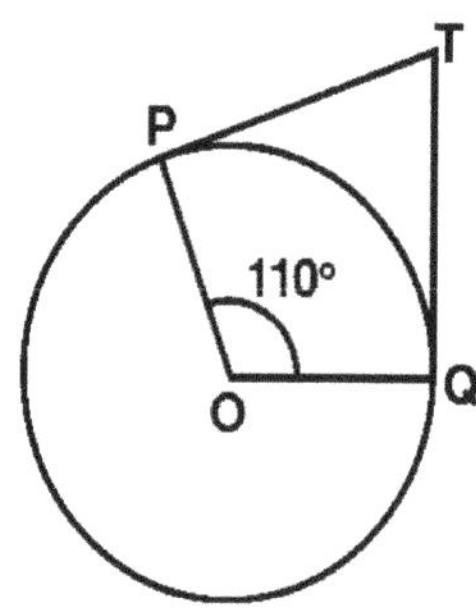

We can see, OP is the radius of the circle to the tangent PT and OQ is the radius to the tangents TQ.

So, $OP \perp PT$ and $TQ \perp OQ$

$\therefore \angle OPT = \angle OQT = 90°$

Now, in the quadrilateral POQT, we know that the sum of the interior angles is 360°

So, $\angle PTQ + \angle POQ + \angle OPT + \angle OQT = 360°$

Now, by putting the respective values, we get,

$\Rightarrow \angle PTQ + 90° + 110° + 90° = 360°$

$\Rightarrow \angle PTQ = 70°$

8. The length of a tangent from a point A at a distance 5 cm from the centre of the circle is 4 cm. The radius of the circle is:

A. 3 cm
B. 5 cm
C. 7 cm
D. 10 cm

Answer: A
Explanation:
As per the given question:

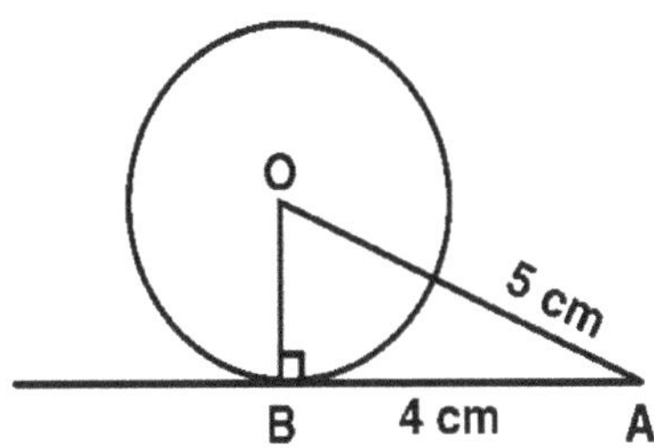

AB is the tangent, drawn on the circle from point A.
So, OB ⊥ AB
Given, OA = 5cm and AB = 4 cm
Now, In △ABO,
$OA^2 = AB^2 + BO^2$ (Using Pythagoras theorem)
⇒ $52 = 42 + BO^2$
⇒ $BO^2 = 25 - 16$
⇒ $BO^2 = 9$
⇒ BO = 3

9. If a parallelogram circumscribes a circle, then it is a:
A. Square
B. Rectangle
C. Rhombus
D. None of the above

Answer: C
Explanation:
If a parallelogram circumscribes a circle, then it is a Rhombus.

10. Two concentric circles are of radii 5 cm and 3 cm. The length of the chord of the larger circle which touches the smaller circle is:
A. 8 cm

B. 10 cm

C. 12 cm

D. 18 cm

Answer: A

Explanation:

As per the given question:

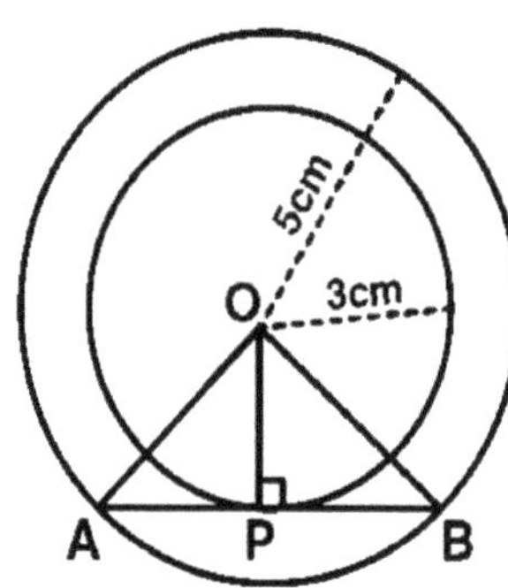

From the above figure, AB is tangent to the smaller circle at point P.

∴ OP ⊥ AB

By Pythagoras theorem, in triangle OPA

$OA^2 = AP^2 + OP^2$

$\Rightarrow 52 = AP^2 + 32$

$\Rightarrow AP^2 = 25 - 9$

$\Rightarrow AP = 4$

Now, as OP ⊥ AB,

Since the perpendicular from the center of the circle bisects the chord, AP will be equal to PB

So, $AB = 2AP = 2 \times 4 = 8$ cm

11. If angle between two radii of a circle is 130°, the angle between the tangents at the ends of the radii is

A. 90°

B. 50°

C. 70°

D. 40°

Answer: B

Explanation:

We know that the sum of the angle between two radii of a circle and the angle between the tangents at the ends of the radii is 180°.

Therefore, the angle between the tangents at the ends of the radii = 180° – 130° = 50°

12. A line intersecting a circle in two points is called a _______.

A. Secant

B. Chord

C. Diameter

D. Tangent

Answer: A

Explanation:

A line intersecting a circle in two points is called a Secant.

13. In the figure below, the pair of tangents AP and AQ drawn from an external point A to a circle with centre O are perpendicular to each other and length of each tangent is 5 cm. Then the radius of the circle is

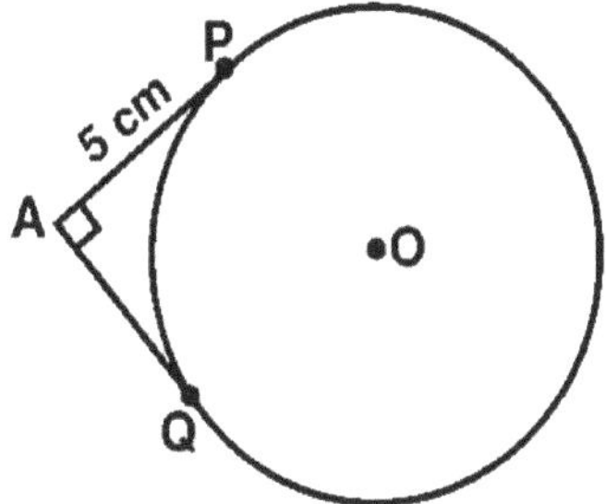

A. 10 cm

B. 7.5 cm

C. 5 cm

D. 2.5 cm

Answer: C

Explanation:

Join OP and OQ.

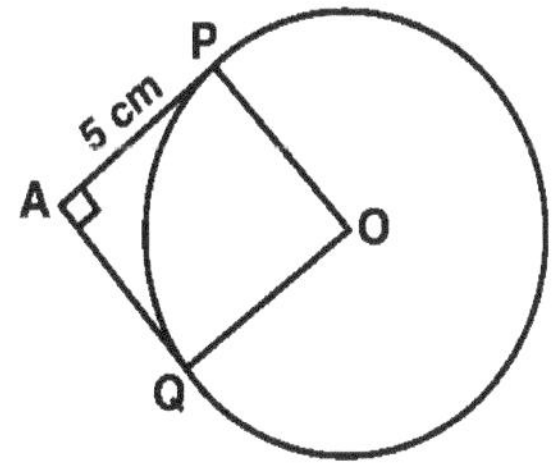

Tangents AP = AQ
In triangle APO and AQO,
AP = AQ
AO = AO (Common)
OP = OQ (radius of same circle)
Thus, ΔAPO ~ ΔAQO.
POQA is a square.
OP = OQ = AP = AQ
So, AP = AQ = 5 Cm
And AP = OP (Proved)
Therefore, radius = OP = 5 cm

14. If two tangents inclined at an angle 60° are drawn to a circle of radius 3 cm, then length of each tangent is equal to

A. (3/2) √3 cm
B. 6 cm
C. 3 cm
D. 3√3 cm

Answer: D
Explanation:

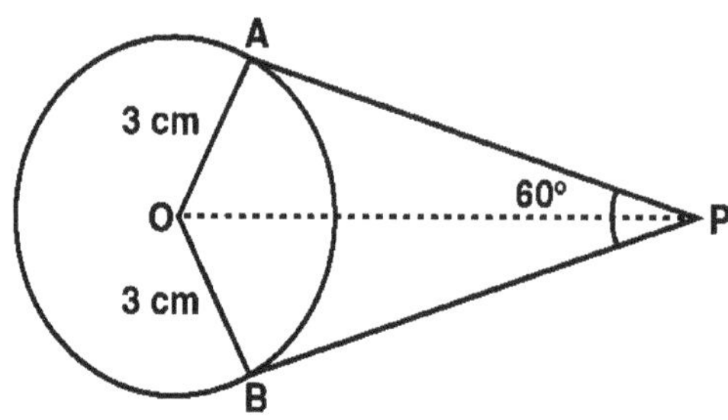

ΔAOP and ΔBOP are congruent.
Therefore, ∠APO = ∠BPO = 60°/2 = 30°
OA is perpendicular to AP.
In right triangle AOP,
tan 30° = OA/AP
1/√3 = 3/AP
AP = 3√3
Hence, the length of the tangent is 3√3 cm.

15. The tangent to a circle is ___________ to the radius through the point of contact.

A. parallel
B. perpendicular
C. perpendicular bisector
D. bisector

Answer: B
Explanation:
The tangent to a circle is perpendicular to the radius through the point of contact.

16. In the figure below, PQ is a chord of a circle and PT is the tangent at P such that ∠QPT = 60°. Then ∠PRQ is equal to

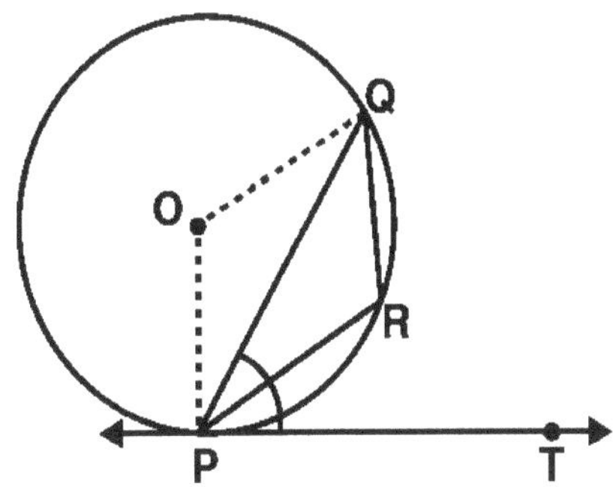

A. 135°
B. 150°
C. 120°
D. 110°

Answer: C
Explanation:
From the given,
∠QPT = 60°
∠OPT = 90°
Thus, ∠OPQ = ∠OQP = 30°, i.e., ∠POQ = 120°.
Also, ∠PRQ = (1/2) reflex ∠POQ
reflex ∠POQ = 360° – 120° = 240°
Therefore, ∠PRQ = (1/2) × 240° = 120°

17. In the below figure, if ∠AOB = 125°, then ∠COD is equal to

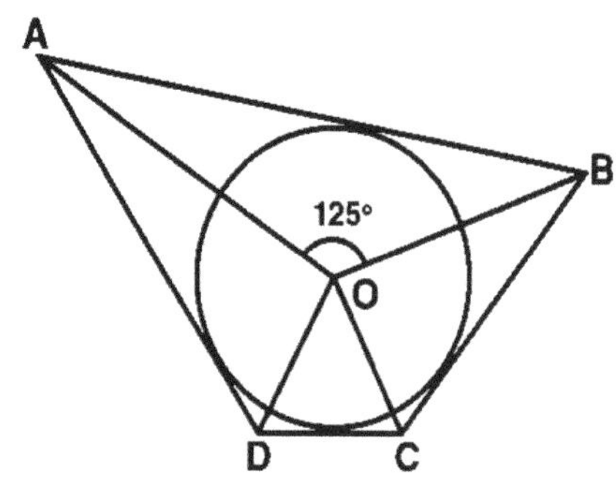

A. 62.5°
B. 45°
C. 35°
D. 55°

Answer: D
Explanation:
ABCD is a quadrilateral circumscribing the circle.
Thus, the opposite sides of a quadrilateral circumscribing a circle subtend supplementary angles at the center of the circle.
∠AOB + ∠COD = 180°
125° + ∠COD = 180°
∠COD = 180° – 125° = 55°

18. In the figure, PQL and PRM are tangents to the circle with centre O at the points Q and R, respectively and S is a point on the circle such that ∠SQL = 50° and ∠SRM = 60°. Then ∠QSR is equal to

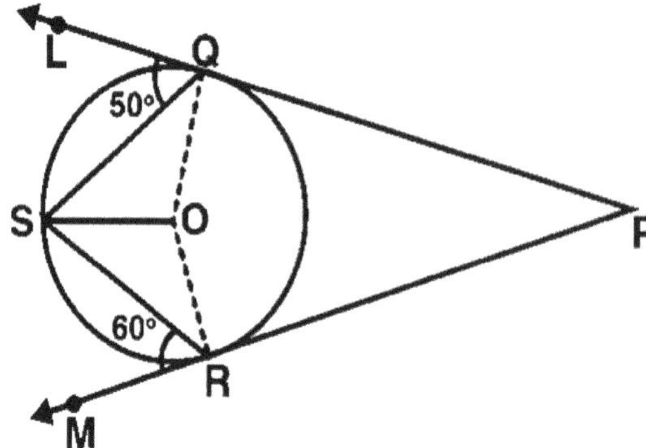

A. 40°
B. 60°
C. 70°
D. 80°

Answer: C

Explanation:

From the given,

∠OSQ = ∠OQS = 90°–50° = 40°

and

∠RSO = ∠SRO = 90° – 60° = 30°

Therefore, ∠QSR = 40° + 30° = 70°.

19. Out of the two concentric circles, the radius of the outer circle is 5cm and the chord AC of length 8 cm is a tangent to the inner circle. The radius of the inner circle will be.

A. 3 cm

B. 4 cm

C. 2.5 cm

D. 2 cm

Answer: A

Explanation:

OA = 5 cm and AC = 8 cm

AC is a chord which touches the inner circle at point B.

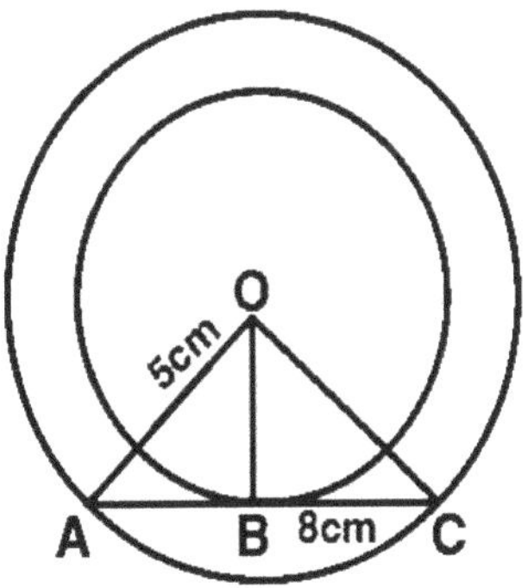

Join OB.

So, OB ⊥ AC

AD = DC = 4 cm {perpendicular line OB bisects the chord}

Thus, in right angled ΔAOB,

$OA^2 = AB^2 + BO^2$

$BO^2 = 52 – 42 = 25 – 16 = 9$

BO = 3 cm

Hence, the radius of the inner circle will be 3 cm.

20. The distance between two parallel tangents of a circle is 18 cm, then the radius of the circle is

A. 8 cm

B. 10 cm

C. 9 cm

D. 7.5 cm

Answer: C

Explanation:

Given,

Distance between two parallel tangents = 18 cm

That means, diameter = 18 cm

Therefore, radius of the circle = 18/2 = 9 cm

21. The distance between two parallel tangents of a circle of radius 4 cm is

A. 2 cm

B. 4 cm

C. 6 cm

D. 8 cm

Answer: D

Explanation:

Here radius, r = 4 cm

Required distance,

AB = OA + OB

= r + r = 2r = 2×4 = 8 cm

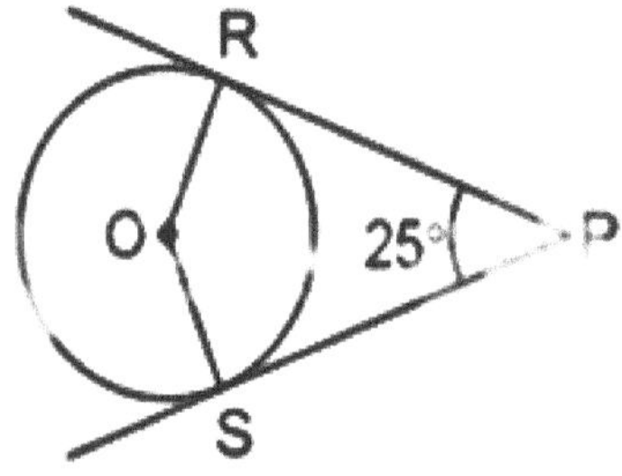

22. In the given figure, if ZRPS = 25°, the value of ZROS is

A. 135°

B. 145°

C. 165°

D. 155°

Answer: D
Explanation:
Since OR ⊥ PR and OS ⊥ PS
$\therefore \angle ORP = \angle OSP = 90°$
In ∠ORPS, $\angle ROS + \angle ORP + \angle RPS + \angle OSP = 360°$
$\angle ROS + 90° + 25° + 90° = 360°$
$\angle ROS = 360° - 205° = 155°$

23. A tangent is drawn from a point at a distance of 17 cm of circle C(0, r) of radius 8 cm. The length of its tangent is.
A. 5 cm
B. 9 cm
C. 15 cm
D. 23 cm

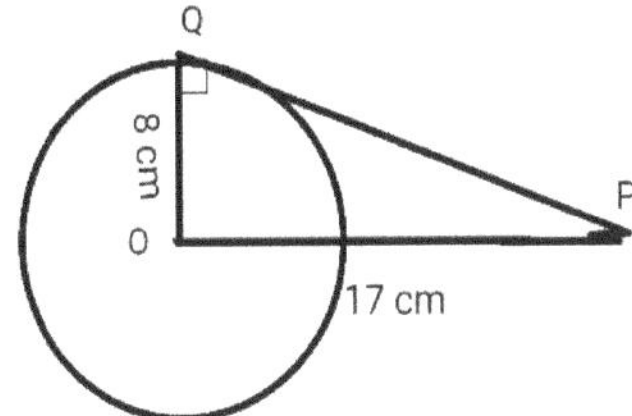

Answer: C
Explanation:
In rt ΔOAP, $AP^2 + OA^2 = OP^2$
$\Rightarrow AP^2 + (8)^2 = (17)^2 \Rightarrow AP^2 + 64 = 289$
$\Rightarrow AP^2 = 289 - 64 = 225$
$\therefore AP = \sqrt{225} = 15$ cm

24. The length of tangents drawn from an external point to the circle
A. are equal
B. are not equal
C. sometimes are equal
D. are not defined

Answer: A
Explanation:

Since the length of tangents drawn from an external point to a circle are equal.

25. Number of tangents drawn at a point of the, circle is/are

A. one

B. two

C. none

D. infinite

Answer: A

Explanation:

There is only one tangent at a point of the circle.

26. The tangents drawn at the extremities of the diameter of a circle are

A. perpendicular

B. parallel

C. equal

D. none of these

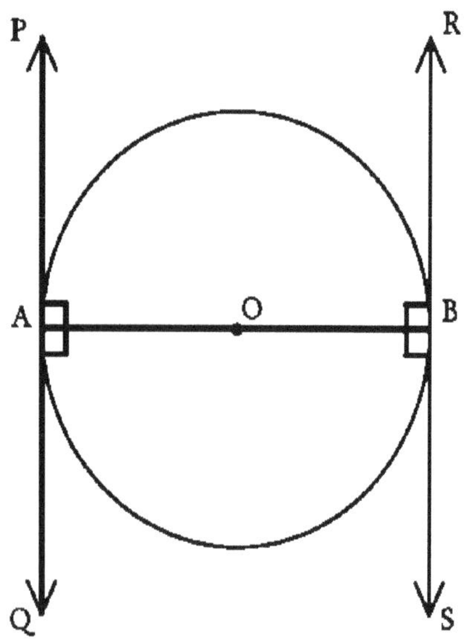

Answer: B

Explanation:

Since OP ⊥ AB and OQ ⊥ CD

∴ Z1 = 90° and Z2 = 90°

⇒ ∠1 = Z2, which are alternate angles.

∴ AB || CD

27. Tangents from an external point to a circle are.

A. equal

B. not equal

C. parallel

D. perpendicular

Answer: A

Explanation:

Tangents from external points to a circle are equal.

28. The length of a tangent drawn from a point at a distance of 10 cm of circle is 8 cm. The radius of the circle is

A. 4 cm

B. 5 cm

C. 6 cm

D. 7 cm

Answer: C

Explanation:

In rt. ΔOAP, we have

$OA^2 + AP^2 = OP^2$

$\Rightarrow OA^2 + (8)^2 = (10)2$

$\Rightarrow OA^2 + 64 = 100$

$\Rightarrow OA^2 = 100 - 64 = 36$

$\therefore OA = \sqrt{36} = 6$ cm

29. In the given figure, CP and CQ are tangents to a circle with centre O. ARB is another tangent touching the circle at R. If CP = 11 cm and BC = 6 cm then the length of BR is

A. 6 cm

B. 5 cm

C. 4 cm

D. 3 cm

Answer: B

Explanation:

Since BQ = BR …(i) [∵ Tangents drawn from external points are equal]

CQ = CP … [Using (i)]
BC + BQ = 11
⇒ 6 + BR = 11
⇒ BR = 11 – 6 = 5 cm

30. From a point P which is at a distance of 13 cm from the centre O of a circle of radius 5 cm, the pair of tangents PQ and PR to the circle are drawn. Then the area of the quadrilateral PQOR is

A. 60 cm^2
B. 65 cm^2
C. 30 cm^2
D. 32.5 cm^2

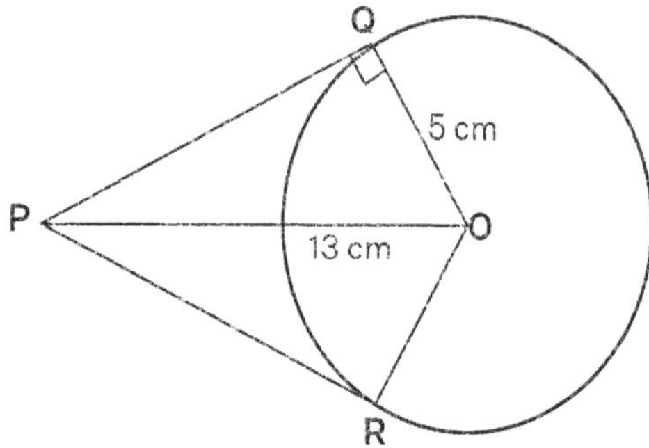

Answer: A
Explanation:
$OP^2 = OQ^2 + PQ^2$
$169 = 25 + PQ^2$
$PQ^2 = 144$
PQ = 12
Area PQOR = area (AOPQ) + area (AOPR)
$= 12 \times 12 \times 5 + 12 \times 12 \times 5 = 60$ cm^2

31. In the given figure, AB and AC are tangents to the circle with centre O such that ∠BAC = 40°, then ∠BOC is equal to

A. 40°
B. 50°
C. 140°
D. 150°

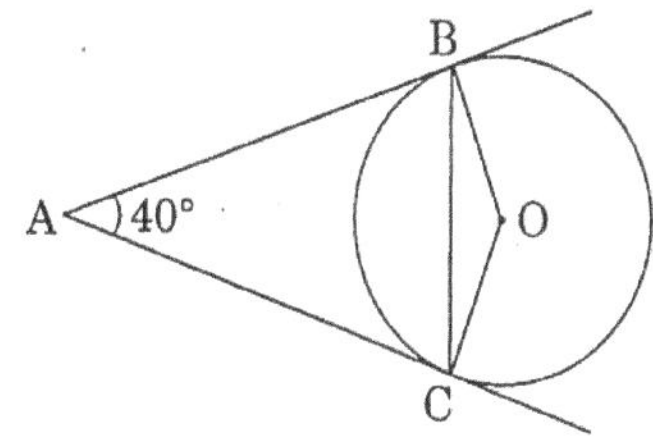

Figure 2

Answer: C

Explanation:

In quadrilateral ABOC

$\angle ABO + \angle BOC + \angle OCA + \angle BAC = 360°$

$\Rightarrow 90° + \angle BOC + 90° + 40° = 360°$

$\Rightarrow \angle BOC = 360° - 220° = 140°$

32. In the given figure, point P is 26 cm away from the centre O of a circle and the length PT of the tangent drawn from P to the circle is 24 cm. Then the radius of the circle is

A. 25 cm

B. 26 cm

C. 24 cm

D. 10 cm

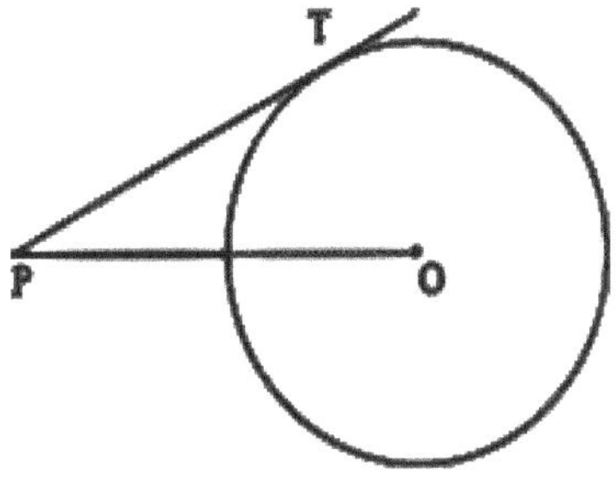

Answer: D

Explanation:

OT is radius and PT is tangent.

$\therefore OT \perp PT$

Now, in AOTP,

$\Rightarrow OP^2 = PT^2 + OT^2$

$\Rightarrow 26^2 = 24^2 + OT^2$

$\Rightarrow 676 - 576 = OT^2$

$\Rightarrow 100 = OT^2$

$\Rightarrow 10 \text{ cm} = OT$

33. A line through point of contact and passing through centre of circle is known as

A. tangent

B. chord

C. normal

D. segment

Answer: C

Explanation:

A line through the point of contract and passing through centre of the circle is known as normal.

34. C (O, r^1) and C (O, r^2) are two concentric circles with $r^1 > r^2$ AB is a chord of C(O, r^1) touching C(O, r^2) at C then

A. AB = r^1

B. AB = r^2

C. AC = BC

D. AB = $r^1 + r^2$

Answer: C

Explanation:

∵ AB touches

C (0, r₂)

∴ OC ⊥ AB

Also, perpendicular from the centre to a chord bisects the chord.

∴ AC = BC

35. Two parallel lines touch the circle at points A and B respectively. If area of the circle is 25 cm^2, then AB is equal to

A. 5 cm

B. 8 cm

C. 10 cm

D. 25 cm

Answer: C

Explanation:

Let radius of circle = R

$\therefore \pi R^2 = 25\pi$

$\Rightarrow R = 5$ cm

$\therefore$ Distance between two parallel tangents = diameter = $2 \times 5 = 10$ cm.

36. In figure if O is centre of a circle, PQ is a chord and the tangent PR at P makes an angle of 50° with PQ, then ∠POQ is equal to

A. 100°

B. 80°

C. 90°

D. 75°

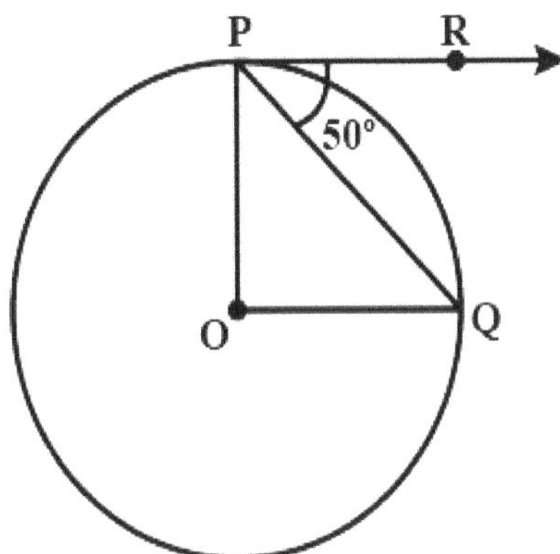

Answer: A

Explanation:

OP ⊥ PR [∵ Tangent and radius are ⊥ to each other at the point of contact]

$\angle OPQ = 90° - 50° = 40°$

OP = OQ [Radii]

$\therefore \angle OPQ = \angle OQP = 40°$

In ΔOPQ,

$\Rightarrow \angle POQ + \angle OPQ + \angle OQP = 180°$

$\Rightarrow \angle POQ + 40° + 40° = 180°$

$\angle POQ = 180° - 80° = 100°$.

37. In figure, O is the centre of a circle, AB is a chord and AT is the tangent at A. If ∠AOB = 100°, then ∠BAT is equal to

A. 100°

B. 40°

C. 50°

D. 90°

Answer: C

Explanation:

$\angle AOB = 100°$

$\angle OAB = \angle OBA$ ($\because$ OA and OB are radii)

Now, in ΔAOB,

$\angle AOB + \angle OAB + \angle OBA = 180°$

(Angle sum property of A)

$\Rightarrow 100° + x + x = 180°$ [Let $\angle OAB = \angle OBA = x$]

$\Rightarrow 2x = 180° - 100°$

$\Rightarrow 2x = 80°$

$\Rightarrow x = 40°$

Also, $\angle OAB + \angle BAT = 90°$

[$\because$ OA is radius and TA is tangent at A]

$\Rightarrow 40° + \angle BAT = 90°$

$\Rightarrow \angle BAT = 50°$

38. In the figure PA and PB are tangents to the circle with centre O. If $\angle APB = 60°$, then $\angle OAB$ is

A. 30°

B. 60°

C. 90°

D. 15°

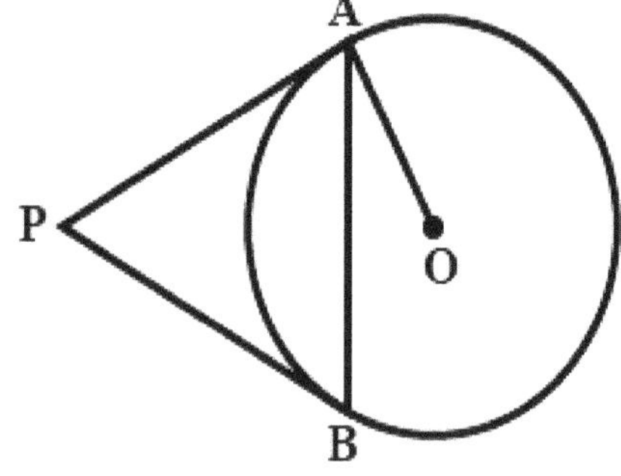

Answer: A

Explanation:

Given $\angle APB = 60°$

$\because \angle APB + \angle PAB + \angle PBA = 180°$

$\Rightarrow APB + x + x = 180°$

[$\because PA = PB \therefore \angle PAB = \angle PBA = x$ (say)]

$\Rightarrow 60° + 2x = 180°$

⇒ 2x = 180° – 60°
⇒ 2x = 120°
⇒ x = 120°2 = 60°
Also, ∠OAP = 90°
⇒ ∠OAB + ∠PAB = 90°
⇒ ∠OAB + 60°= 90°
⇒ ∠OAB = 30°

39. In the given figure, TP and TQ are two tangents to a circle with centre O, such that ∠POQ = 110°. Then ∠PTQ is equal to

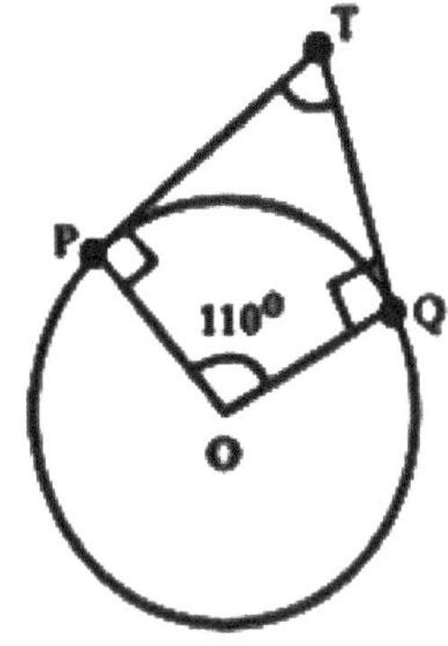

A. 55°
B. 70°
C. 110°
D. 90°

Answer: B
Explanation:
In quadrilateral POQT,
∠PTQ + ∠TPO + ∠TQO + ∠POQ
= 360°
⇒ ∠PTQ + 90° + 90° + 110° = 360°
⇒ ∠PTQ + 290° = 360°
⇒ ∠PTQ = 360° – 290° = 70°

40. In figurc, PQ and PR are tangents to a circle with centre A. If ∠QPA−27°, then ∠QAR equals to
A. 63°
B. 153°
C. 110°

D. 90°

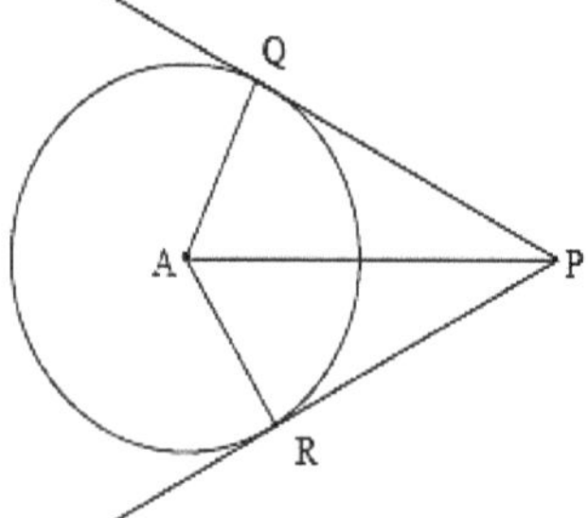

Answer: C

Explanation:

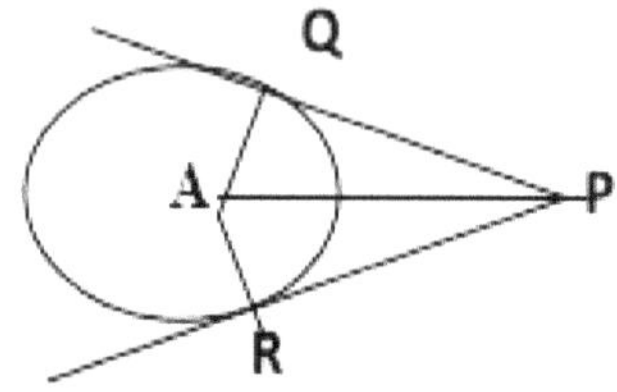

∠QPA = ∠RPA

[∵ ΔAQP ≅ ΔARP (RHS congruence rule)]

⇒ ∠RPA = 27°

∴ ∠QPR = ∠QPA + ∠RPA

= 27° + 27° = 54°

Now,

∠QAR + ∠AQP + ∠ARP + ∠QPR = 360°

⇒ ∠QAR = 90° + 90° + 54° = 360°

⇒ ∠QAR = 360° – 234° = 126°

41. In figure if PQR is the tangent to a circle at Q whose centre is O, AB is a chord parallel to PR and ∠BQR = 70°, then ∠AQB is equal to

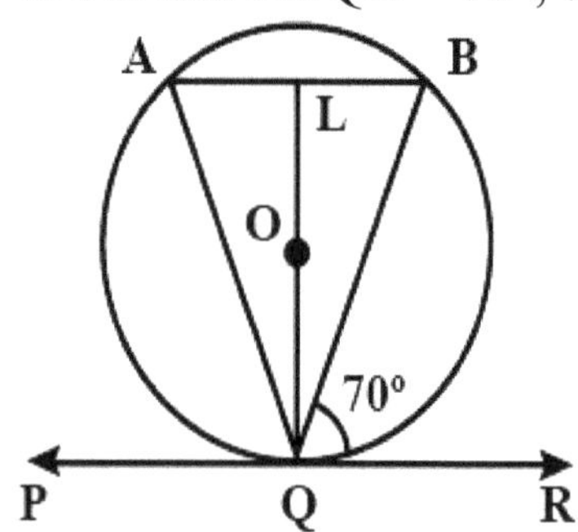

A. 20°

B. 40°

C. 35°

D. 45°

Answer: B

Explanation:

AB || PR

∴ ∠ABQ =∠BQR

[Alternate interior angles]

⇒ ∠ABQ = 70°

Also, ∠BQR = ∠BAQ [Angles in alternate segment]

⇒ ∠BAQ = 70°

In ΔAQB,

∠BAQ + ∠ABQ + ∠AQB = 180°

⇒ 70° + 70° + ∠AQB = 180°

⇒ ∠AQB = 180° – 140° = 40°.

42. If angle between two radii of a circle is 130°, then the angle between the tangents at the ends of the radii is:

A. 90°

B. 50°

C. 70°

D. 40°

Answer: B

Explanation:

If the angle between two radii of a circle is 130°, then the angle between tangents is 180° – 130° = 50°. (By the properties of circles and tangents)

43. If angle between two tangents drawn from a point P to a circle of radius 'a'and centre 'O' is 90°, then OP =

A. $2a\sqrt{2}$

B. $a\sqrt{2}$

C. $a/\sqrt{2}$

D. $5a\sqrt{2}$

Answer: B

Explanation:

From point P, two tangents are drawn.

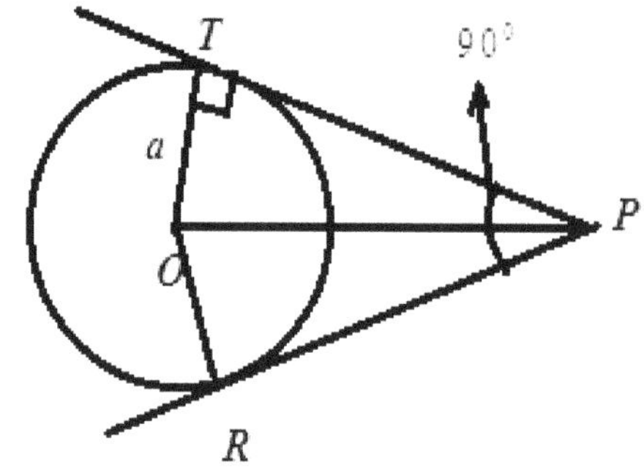

OT = a (given)

Also line OP bisects the RPT

Therefore,

TPO = RPO = 45°

Also

OT is perpendicular to PT

In right triangle OTP

sin 45° = OT/OP

⇒ $1/\sqrt{2} = a/OP$

⇒ $OP = a\sqrt{2}$

44. The length of tangent from an external point on a circle is

A. always greater than the radius of the circle.

B. always less than the radius of the circle.

C. may or may not be greater than the radius of circle

D. None of these.

Answer: C

Explanation:

Observe the figure,

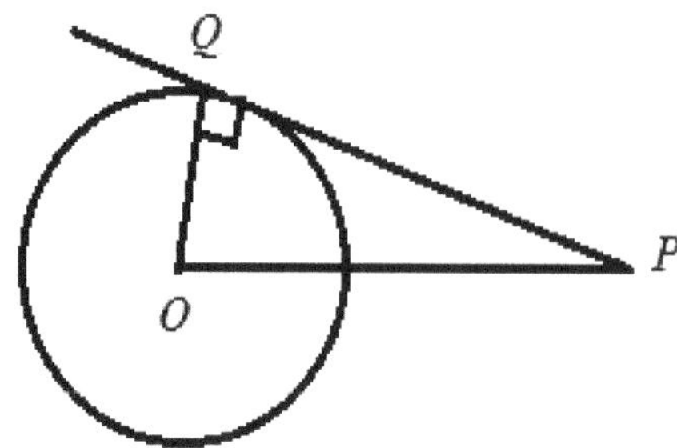

In figure OQ is the radius and QP is the tangent.

For right triangle OQP, radius and tangents are two smaller sides, smaller than hypotenuse OP.

Also, the length of tangent depends upon the distance of external point from circle. Thus, The length of tangent from an external point on a circle may or may not be greater than the radius of circle.

45. At one end A of a diameter AB of a circle of radius 5 cm, tangent XAY is drawn to the circle. The length of the chord CD parallel to XY and at a distance 8 cm from A is

A. 4 cm

B. 5 cm

C. 6 cm

D. 8 cm

Answer: D

Explanation:

Observe the figure,

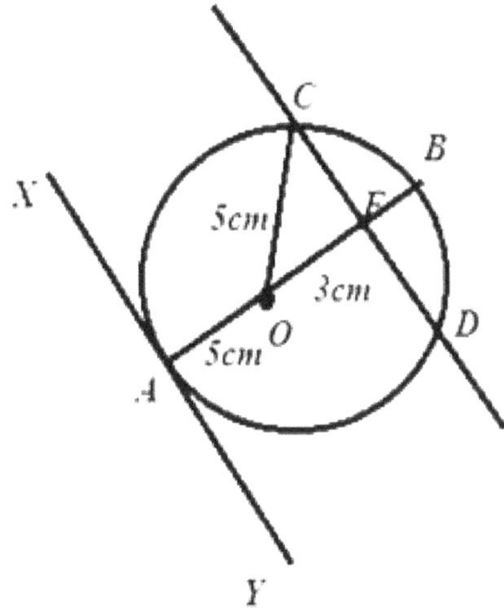

Since OC = OA= radius =5cm

Therefore

OE = AE – AO

OE = 8 – 5

OE = 3 cm

In right triangle OEC

$OC^2 = OE^2 + CE^2$

$\Rightarrow 5^2 = 3^2 + CE^2$

$\Rightarrow CE^2 = 25 - 9$

$\Rightarrow CE^2 = 16$

$\Rightarrow CE = 4$

Therefore, length of chord CD = 2×4 = 8cm

46. In the following figure, if O is the centre of a circle, PQ is a chord and the tangent PR at P makes an angle of 50° with PQ, then ∠POQ is equal to

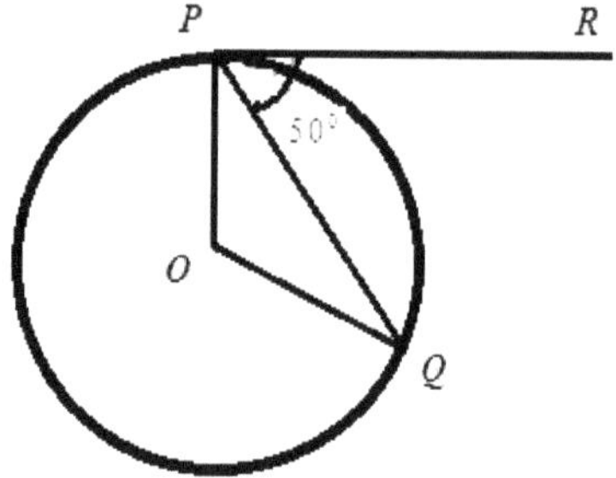

A. 100°
B. 80°
C. 90°
D. 75°

Answer: A
Explanation:
From figure using properties of circle and tangents
∠OPQ = 90° – 50°
∠OPQ = 40°
OP = OQ = radius
So (∠OPQ) = ∠OQP = 40°
Now In ΔPOQ
∠POQ = 180° - (∠OPQ + ∠OQP)
∠POQ = 180° - (40° + 40°)
∠POQ = 100°

47. In the following figure, PA and PB are tangents from a point P to a circle with centre O. Then the quadrilateral OAPB must be a

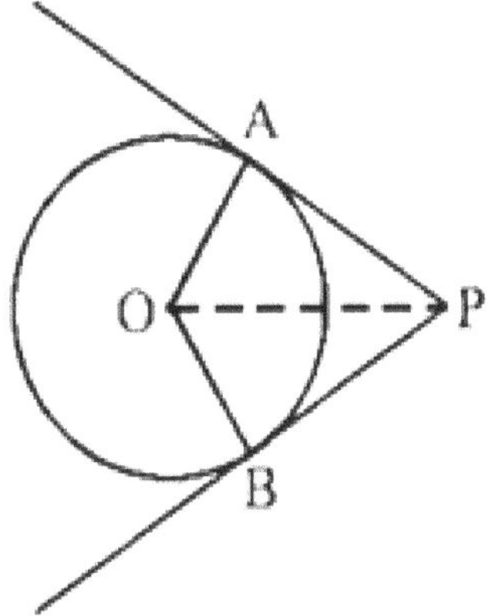

A. Square
B. Rhombus
C. Cyclic quadrilateral
D. Parallelogram

Answer: C
Explanation:
Since tangent and radius intersect at right angle,
So,
$\angle OAP = \angle OBP = 90°$
$\Rightarrow \angle OAP + \angle OBP = 90° + 90° = 180°$
Which are opposite angles of quadrilateral OAPB
So the sum of remaining two angles is also 180°
Therefore, Quad OAPB is cyclic Quadrilateral.

48. If a chord AB subtends an angle of 60° at the centre of a circle, then angle between the tangents at A and B is:
A. 60°
B. 120°
C. 80°
D. 100°

Answer: A
Explanation:
Observe the figure

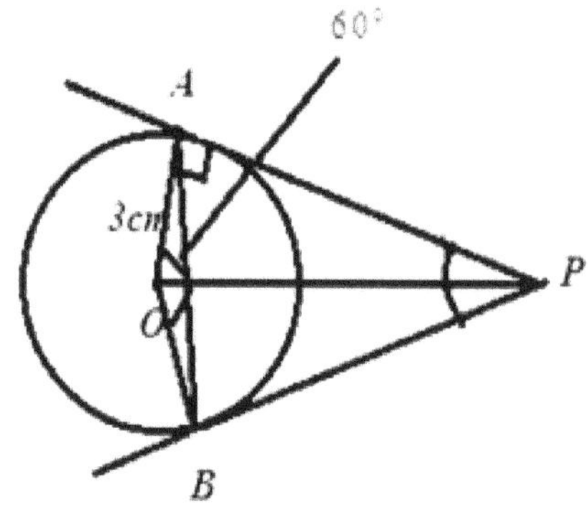

Using properties of circles and tangents, angle between tangents is:

= 180° - 60°

= 120°

49. If two tangents inclined at an angle 60° are drawn to a circle of radius 3 cm, then length of each tangent is equal to

A. 2√3 cm

B. 6√3 cm

C. 3√3 cm

D. 3 cm

Answer: C

Explanation:

Let P be an external point from which pair of tangents are drawn as shown in the figure given below:

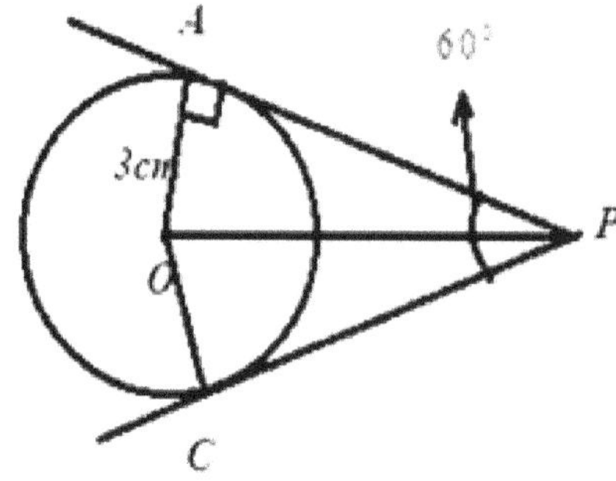

Join OA and OP

Also OP is a bisector line of ∠APC

∠APO = ∠CPO = 30°

OA ⊥ AP

Therefore, in triangle OAP

tan30° = OA/AP

1/√3 = 3/AP

AP = 3√3cm

MIXTURE AND ALLIGATION

Introduction

Mixture and alligation is a mathematical technique used to solve problems related to combining different elements or ingredients of varying strengths or concentrations to create a mixture of a desired strength or concentration. It is commonly used in fields such as chemistry, physics, and finance.

In simple terms, mixture refers to the combination of two or more different substances or ingredients, while alligation refers to the process of finding the average value of the concentration of a mixture, when its constituents have different concentrations.

Mixture and alligation involves the use of a formula that takes into account the quantities and concentrations of the various elements or ingredients involved in the mixture. This formula is based on the principle of proportionality, which states that the ratio of the quantities of the constituents in the mixture is equal to the ratio of their respective strengths or concentrations.

By using mixture and alligation, we can determine the quantities of each ingredient needed to create a mixture of a desired concentration, or we can calculate the concentration of a mixture based on the concentrations of its individual components.

Rules Of Mixture and Alligation:

The following are the rules of mixture and alligation:

1. In a simple mixture of two or more ingredients, the proportion of each ingredient in the final mixture is directly proportional to its quantity and strength.

2. If the ratio of the quantities of two ingredients in a mixture is given, and the strength of one of the ingredients is also given, then the strength of the other ingredient can be calculated using alligation.

3. If the ratio of the strengths of two ingredients in a mixture is given, and the quantity of one of the ingredients is also given, then the quantity of the other ingredient can be calculated using alligation.

4. If two or more mixtures of different strengths are mixed together to create a final mixture of a desired strength, then alligation can be used to determine the quantities of each mixture required to create the final mixture.

5. If a mixture of a certain strength is to be obtained by mixing two or more ingredients of different strengths, then alligation can be used to determine the quantities of each ingredient required to create the final mixture.

Method 1 (formula method): It is given as-

$$\frac{\text{Quantity of Cheaper}}{\text{Quantity of Dearer}} = \frac{\text{Cost price of Dearer} - \text{Mean Price}}{\text{Mean Price} - \text{Cost price of Cheaper}}$$

Method 2 (Diagram method): The above method can be expressed using a diagram which will be more convenient to understand-

Cost price of Cheaper 'C' | Cost price of Dearer 'D'

Mean Price 'M'

Quantity of Cheaper 'D – M' | Quantity of Dearer 'M – C'

Types Of Mixture And Alligation

There are two types of mixture and alligation:

1. Simple Mixture and Alligation: A simple mixture and alligation problem involves mixing two or more ingredients of different strengths or concentrations to create a mixture of a desired strength or concentration. In a simple mixture problem, the ratio of the quantities of the ingredients in the final mixture is directly proportional to their strengths or concentrations.

For example, if we want to create a mixture of alcohol and water with a concentration of 40%, and we have alcohol with a strength of 60% and water with a strength of 10%, we can use mixture and alligation to determine the quantities of alcohol and water required to create the final mixture.

2. Compound Mixture and Alligation: A compound mixture and alligation problem involves mixing two or more mixtures of different strengths or concentrations to create a final mixture of a desired strength or concentration. In a compound mixture problem, alligation is used to determine the quantities of each mixture required to create the final mixture.

   For example, if we have two mixtures of alcohol and water, one with a strength of 40% and the other with a strength of 80%, and we want to create a final mixture with a strength of 60%, we can use mixture and alligation to determine the quantities of each mixture required to create the final mixture.

Fundamentals Of Mixture And Alligation

The fundamentals of mixture and alligation are based on the following principles:

1. The principle of proportionality: The ratio of the quantities of the ingredients in a mixture is directly proportional to their strengths or concentrations. This principle forms the basis of alligation.

2. The principle of mean value: In a mixture of two or more ingredients, the mean value of the strength or concentration of the mixture is equal to the weighted average of the strengths or concentrations of the individual ingredients.

3. The principle of equivalent values: Two or more mixtures of different strengths or concentrations can be considered equivalent if they have the same mean value of strength or concentration.

Merits And Demerits

Merits:

1. Mixture and alligation are powerful tools for solving problems related to mixing and blending of different substances or ingredients, and can be applied to a wide range of

fields including chemistry, physics, engineering, and economics.

2. Mixture and alligation provide a systematic approach to solving complex mixture problems, making it easier to understand and calculate the proportions of different ingredients required to create a mixture of a desired strength or concentration.

3. Mixture and alligation provide a graphical representation of the process, which can help in visualizing the problem and identifying the correct solution.

4. Mixture and alligation are simple and easy to understand and can be applied to both simple and complex mixture problems.

Demerits:

1. Mixture and alligation can be time-consuming, especially for complex problems, and require a certain level of mathematical knowledge and skill.

2. Mixture and alligation assume that the ingredients or components being mixed are homogeneous and do not take into account any variation in the properties of the ingredients or components.

3. Mixture and alligation can sometimes provide approximate solutions rather than exact solutions, which can result in some degree of error in the final result.

Method of Mixture and Alligation

The method of mixture and alligation is a mathematical technique used to solve problems related to the mixing of different substances or ingredients with different strengths or concentrations. The method involves the following steps:

1. Identify the components of the mixture and their respective strengths or concentrations.

2. Draw an alligation diagram, which is a graphical representation of the process of alligation. The diagram consists of a straight line with marks or dots representing the different components and their strengths or concentrations.

3. Determine the mean value, which is the average strength or concentration of the final mixture. To do this, find the weighted average of the strengths or concentrations of the

individual components, where the weights are the quantities of each component in the mixture.

4. Determine the ratios of the components required to create the final mixture of the desired strength or concentration. To do this, draw a line from the mean value on the alligation diagram to the desired strength or concentration and mark the points where the line intersects the dots representing the components.

5. Use the ratios to calculate the quantities of each component required to create the final mixture. To do this, multiply the ratio of each component by the total quantity of the mixture.

6. Check the calculations and ensure that the quantities of each component add up to the total quantity of the mixture.

MULTIPLE CHOICE QUESTIONS

1. An alloy has Gold and Copper in ratio 3:4. Another alloy has Gold and Copper in ratio 5:3. In what ratio they should be mixed so that the final mixture has Gold and Copper in ratio 5:4?

A. 17:32

B. 9:16

C. 71:128

D. 35:64

Answer: D

Explanation:

Let Mkg of the first alloy and Nkg of the second alloy be mixed.

$$\text{Amount of Gold in mixture } = \frac{3M}{7} + \frac{5\text{ N}}{8}$$

$$\text{Amount of Copper in mixture } = \frac{4M}{7} + \frac{3N}{8}$$

$$\Rightarrow \frac{\frac{3M}{7} + \frac{5N}{8}}{\frac{4M}{7} + \frac{3N}{8}} = \frac{5}{4}$$

$$\Rightarrow \frac{12M}{7} + \frac{20N}{8} = \frac{20M}{7} + \frac{15N}{8}$$

$$\frac{5N}{8} = \frac{8M}{7}$$

$$\Rightarrow \frac{M}{N} = \frac{35}{64}$$

$\therefore$ The ratio should be 35: 64

2. A mixture contains milk and water in the ratio 9:8. If 10 liters of water is added to it, the ratio of milk and water becomes 51:47. Find the original quantity of milk in the mixture.

A. 306 liters

B. 272liters

C. 282 liters

D. 305 liters

Answer: A

Explanation:

Let the quantity of milk and water be $9x$ liters and $8x$ liters respectively.

As per the given details,

$$\frac{9x}{8x+10} = \frac{51}{47}$$

$\Rightarrow 423x = 408x + 510$

$\Rightarrow 423x - 408x = 510$

$\Rightarrow 15x = 510$

$\Rightarrow x = \frac{510}{15}$

$\Rightarrow x = 34$

$\therefore$ Original quantity of milk in the mixture = $9x = 9 \times 34 = 306$ liters

3. A vessel contains 2.5 liters of water and 10 liters of milk. 20% of the contents of the vessel are removed. To the remaining contents, x liters of water is added to reverse the ratio of water and milk. Then y liter of milk is added again to reverse the ratio of water and milk. Find y.

A. 120
B. 200
C. 150
D. 100

Answer: A

Explanation:

Given:

The initial quantity of water in vessel = 2.5 liters

And the initial quantity of milk in vessel = 10 liters

The ratio of milk and water = $10: 2.5 = 4: 1$

Amount of mixture removed = $\left(\frac{20}{100}\right) \times (10 + 2.5) = \left(\frac{1}{5}\right) \times 12.5 = 2.5$ litres

Amount of milk removed = $2.5 \times \left(\frac{4}{5}\right) = 2$ litres

Amount of water removed = $2.5 \times \left(\frac{1}{5}\right) = 0.5$ litres

Now, After adding x litres of water the ratio of milk and water get reversed,

$$\frac{(10-2)}{(2.5-0.5+x)} = \frac{1}{4}$$

$\Rightarrow \frac{8}{(2+x)} = \frac{1}{4}$

$\Rightarrow 8 \times 4 = 2 + x$
$\Rightarrow x = 32 - 2$
$\Rightarrow x = 30$
Now, Quantity of water = $(2.5 - 0.5 + 30)$ liters = 32 liters
And, Quantity of milk = $(10 - 2)$ liters = 8 liters
Then, After adding y litres of milk the ratio of milk and water get reversed,

$$\frac{(8+y)}{32} = \frac{4}{1}$$

$\Rightarrow 8 + y = 32 \times 4$
$\Rightarrow 8 + y = 128$
$\Rightarrow y = 120$
$\therefore$ The value of y is 120.

4. Several litres of milk was drawn off a 27 litre container full of milk which was replaced by an equal amount of water. The same volume of the mixture was drawn off again and replaced with water. Finally, the container contained 12 litres of milk. How much milk was initially drawn?

A. 8 litres
B. 9 litres
C. 10 litres
D. 12 litres

Answer: B
Explanation:
Let $\boldsymbol{x}$ litres of milk was drawn initially and replaced with water.
$\therefore$ The container now contained $(27 - x)$ litres of milk and x litres of water.
An again x litre of milk was drawn.
$\therefore$ Milk drawn from the container in second time = $x \times \frac{(27-x)}{27}$ litres
$\therefore$ Total milk drawn = $\mathrm{x} + \left[(27 - \mathrm{x}) \times \frac{x}{27}\right]$
Total milk left = $27 - x - \left[(27 - x) \times \frac{x}{27}\right]$

$$\Rightarrow 12 = 27 - x - \left[(27 - x) \times \frac{x}{27}\right]$$

$$\Rightarrow 15 = x + \left[(27 - x) \times \frac{x}{27}\right]$$

$$\Rightarrow 15 = x + x - \frac{x^2}{27}$$

$$\Rightarrow 15 = 2x - \frac{x^2}{27}$$
$\Rightarrow 405 = 54x - x^2$
$\Rightarrow x^2 - 54x + 405 = 0$
$\Rightarrow x^2 - 45x - 9x + 405 = 0$
$\Rightarrow x(x - 45) - 9(x - 45) = 0$
$\Rightarrow (x - 45)(x - 9) = 0$
$\Rightarrow x = 45$ or $x = 9$
$\because x$ can't be more then 27.
$\therefore$ 9 litre of milk was drawn initially.

5. 18 litres of a mixture contains milk and water in the ratio $5:4$. How much milk should be added to this mixture, so that the resulting mixture has milk and water in the ratio $7:4$?
A. 4 litres
B. 5 litres
C. 3 litre
D. 2 litres

Answer: A
Explanation:
Let the quantity of milk and water be $5x$ litres and $4x$ litres respectively.
As per the given details,
$5x + 4x = 18$
$\Rightarrow 9x = 18$
$\Rightarrow x = 2$
Original quantity of milk in the mixture $= 5x = 5 \times 2 = 10$ litres
Original quantity of water in the mixture $= 4x = 4 \times 2 = 8$ litres
Also, let the amount of milk to be added be y.
$$\Rightarrow \frac{10 + y}{8} = \frac{7}{4}$$
$\Rightarrow 10 + y = 14$
$\Rightarrow y = 4$ litres

6. A 65 liters solution contained honey and sugar in the ratio 4: 1.15 liters of the mixture was spilled by the housemaid and to avoid being scolded, she replaced that spilled amount but with pure honey. What is the ratio of honey and sugar in the mixture?
A. 6:1
B. 5:1
C. 11:2

D. 14:3

Answer: C
Explanation:
Total volume of mixture = 65 litres

Total volume of honey initially = $65 \times \left(\frac{4}{5}\right) = 52$ litres

Total volume of sugar in mixture = 13 litres

After removing 15 litres of the mixture, honey and sugar are also removed proportionately.
It means 12 litres of honey and 3 litres of sugar is removed.

After replacement, amount of honey in mixture = $52 - 12 + 15 = 55$ litres

Amount of sugar in the mixture = $13 - 3 = 10$ litres

∴ New ratio is $55:10 = 11:2$

7. Two vessels contain milk and water in the ratio 3:1 and 5:3. Find the ratio on which these two must be mixed to get a new mixture in which the ratio of milk to water becomes 2:1.

A. $2:3$
B. $4:5$
C. $3:1$
D. $1:2$

Answer: D
Explanation:
Milk in the first vessel = $\frac{3}{4}$ of mixture

Milk in the second vessel = $\frac{5}{8}$ of mixture

Given that milk in the resultant mixture be $\left(\frac{2}{3}\right)$ of the mixture.

Suppose 1st mixture: 2nd mixture = $1:x$

Total volume of new mixture = $1 + x$

Milk in first vessel + Milk in the second vessel = Milk in the resultant mixture

$$\left\{\left(\frac{3}{4}\times 1\right)\right\} + \left\{\left(\frac{5}{8}\right)\times x\right\} = \left\{(1+x)\times\left(\frac{2}{3}\right)\right\}$$

$$\Rightarrow \frac{3}{4} + \frac{5x}{8} = \frac{2}{3} + \frac{2x}{3x}$$

$$\Rightarrow \frac{3}{4} - \frac{2}{3} = \frac{2x}{3} - \frac{5x}{8}$$

$$\Rightarrow \frac{(9-8)}{12} = \frac{(16x - 15x)}{24}$$

$\Rightarrow x = 2$

$\therefore$ Required ratio $= 1:2$

8. A mixture of 343 litres of wine and water is to be distributed in the ratio of $5:2$. How much more water should be added so that the new mixture contains wine and water in the ratio of $5:3$?

A. 49 litres
B. 30 litres
C. 40 litres
D. 39 litres

Answer: A
Explanation:

The initial quantity of mixture $= 343$ litres

Initial ratio of mixture $= 5:2$

The final ratio of mixture $= 5:3$

Let initial quantity of wine and water be $5x$ and $2x$.

$5x + 2x = 343$

$\Rightarrow 7x = 343$

$\Rightarrow x = 49$

Initial quantity of wine $= 5x$

$= 5 \times 49$

$= 245$ litres

Initial quantity of sugar $= 2x$

$= 2 \times 49$

$= 98$ litres

Let the water to be added in new mixture be x litres.

According to the question,

$$\frac{245}{(98 + x)} = \frac{5}{3}$$

$\Rightarrow 245 \times 3 = 5(98 + x)$

$\Rightarrow 735 = 490 + 5x$

$\Rightarrow 5x = 245$

$\Rightarrow x = 49$ litres

∴ The quantity of water added is 49 litres.

9. In a mixture, the ratio of alcohol and water is 6: 5. When 22 liters mixture are replaced by water, the ratio becomes 9: 13. Find the quantity of alcohol after replacement.
A. 40 litres
B. 42 litres
C. 36 litres
D. 34 litres

Answer: C
Explanation:
Given:
Alcohol: Water = 6: 5
22 liters mixture are replaced by water.
Let alcohol = $6x$ and water = $5x$
In 21-liter mixture, alcohol = $\left(\frac{6}{11}\right) \times 21 = 12$ liter
And water = $\left(\frac{5}{11}\right) \times 22 = 10$ liter
According to the question.
$(6x - 12):(5x - 10 + 22) = 9:13$
$\Rightarrow 13(6x - 12) = 9(5x + 12)$
$\Rightarrow 78x - 156 = 45x + 108$
$\Rightarrow 78x - 45x = 108 + 156$
$\Rightarrow 33x = 264$
$\Rightarrow x = 8$
So, alcohol after replacement = $6 \times 8 - 12 = 36$ liter
∴ The quantity of alcohol after the replacement is 36 liter.

10. There is a 120-liter mixture of vinegar and water. The ratio of vinegar to water is 7: 5. A shopkeeper mixes a certain amount of water in order to make the ratio of vinegar to water 5: 6. The new quantity of water is what percentage of the original quantity of water in the mixture.
A. 156%
B. 145%
C. 165%

D. 168%

Answer: D
Explanation:
Given:
Total mixture = 120 liter
Ratio of initial Vinegar to Water = 7: 5
Ratio of new Vinegar to Water = 5: 6
The initial quantity of vinegar = $\left(\frac{7}{12}\right) \times 120 = 70$ liter
The initial quantity of water = $\left(\frac{5}{12}\right) \times 120 = 50$ liter
According to the question,
$$\frac{70}{(50+x)} = \frac{5}{6}$$
⇒ x = 84 − 50 = 34 liter
Required Percentage = $\left[\frac{(50+34)}{50}\right] \times 100 = 168\%$
∴ The new quantity of water in the mixture is 168%.

11. A container contains 30 liters of alcohol. 3 liters of alcohol are taken out and replaced by an equal amount of water. The same process is repeated 2 times more. How much alcohol is left in the container now?
A. 23.45 liters
B. 12.34 liters
C. 21.87 liters
D. 12.56 liters

Answer: C
Explanation:
Given:
Quantity of alcohol = 30 liters
Quantity of A left = Quantity of A originally present
$\times \left[1 - \left(\frac{R}{Q}\right)\right]^n$
Where R, Q, and n is the quantity taken out, the original quantity of the product and process repeated respectively:
Quantity of alcohol left = $30 \times \left[1 - \left(\frac{3}{30}\right)\right]^3$

$= 30 \times \left(\frac{9}{10}\right)^3$
$= \frac{(3 \times 729)}{100}$
$= 21.87$ liters

12. In a mixture, there is 63 litres of water and 77 litres of milk. Some quantity of the mixture is taken out. After that 16 litres of water and 4 litres of milk are added in to the mixture, so that quantity of water and milk are the same in the mixture. Find the total quantity of mixture when some amount of mixture taken out.
A. 90 litres
B. 130 litres
C. 120 litres
D. 100 litres

Answer: C
Explanation:
Given:
Total quantity of mixture $= 63 + 77 = 140$ litres
Let quantity of mixture taken out be a litres.
Percentage Quantity of water in mixture $= \frac{63}{140} \times 100 = 45\%$
Percentage quantity of alcohol in mixture $= \frac{77}{140} \times 100 = 55\%$
Quantity of water in mixture after addition $= 63 - \text{a} \times \frac{45}{100} + 16$
Quantity of milk in mixture after addition $= 77 - \text{a} \times \frac{55}{100} + 4$
Then,
$63 - a \times \frac{45}{100} + 16 = 77 - a \times \frac{55}{100} + 4$
$\Rightarrow a = 20$
$\therefore$ Total quantity of mixture after 20 litres of mixture taken out $= 140 - 20 = 120$ litres

13. A solution of milk and water is to be diluted by adding water till the ratio gets reversed. The amount of water added is equal to the initial quantity of the mixture. If in the initial mixture the quantity of milk was 8 litres, find the quantity of water added.
A. 15 litres
B. 20 litres
C. 12 litres
D. 21 litres

Answer: C
Explanation:
Given:
Initial quantity of milk = 8 liters
Let the quantity of milk and water be m and w respectively.
Now,
$$\frac{m}{(w + m + w)} = \frac{w}{m}$$
$$\Rightarrow \frac{m}{(m + 2w)} = \frac{w}{m}$$
Now,

Initial quantity of milk = 8 litres

$64 = w(8 + 2w)$

$\Rightarrow 32 = w(4 + w)$

$\Rightarrow 32 = 4w + w^2$

$\Rightarrow w = 4$

$\therefore$ Amount of water added $= m + w = 12$ litres

14. In a container the ratio of water and milk is $4:5$. If the 15 litres of water is taken out and 21 litres of milk is added then the ratio of water and milk changes to $15:32$. Find the initial quantity (in litres) of water in the container.
A. 45
B. 30
C. 65
D. 60

Answer: D
Explanation:
Given:
The ratio of water and milk is $4:5$
The final ratio is $15:32$
Let the initial quantity of water and milk in the vessel be $4x$ and $5x$ respectively.
According to the question,
$$\frac{4x - 15}{5x + 21} = \frac{15}{32}$$

$\Rightarrow 128x - 480 = 75x + 315$
$\Rightarrow 53x = 795$
$\Rightarrow x = 15$
Initial quantity of water in the vessel = $4x = 4 \times 15 = 60$ litres

∴ Initial quantity of water in the vessel is 60 litres.

15. Twenty litres of a milk solution having 24% milk and remaining water. How many litres of water must be added to make it a 20% solution of milk?
A. 3 litres
B. 4 litres
C. 6 litres
D. 8 litres

Answer: B
Explanation:
Given:
The initial amount of solution is 20 litres.
The initial amount of milk = $\frac{24}{100} \times 20 = \frac{24}{5}$
The initial amount of water = $\frac{(100-24)}{100} \times 20 = \frac{76}{5}$
Let the amount of water added be x.
According to the question,

$$\frac{\frac{24}{5}}{\left(\frac{76}{5} + x\right)} = \frac{20}{80}$$

$$\Rightarrow \frac{\frac{24}{5}}{\left(\frac{76}{5} + x\right)} = \frac{1}{4}$$

$$\Rightarrow \frac{20}{5} = x$$

$\Rightarrow x = 4$
The amount of water added is 4 litres.

16. In a mixture of milk & water in ratio 4: 1. Some water is added to make the quantity of milk and water equal. Find the quantity of water added in percentage?
A. 40%
B. 36.5%
C. 37%

D. 37.5%

Answer: D

Explanation:

Given:

Ratio of Milk & Water = 4: 1

According to the question,

Water in the mixture = $\frac{1}{5}$

Also,

$\left(\frac{1}{5}\right) \times 100\% = 20\%$

In the final mixture,

The quantity of milk and water = 50%: 50%

Using allegation,

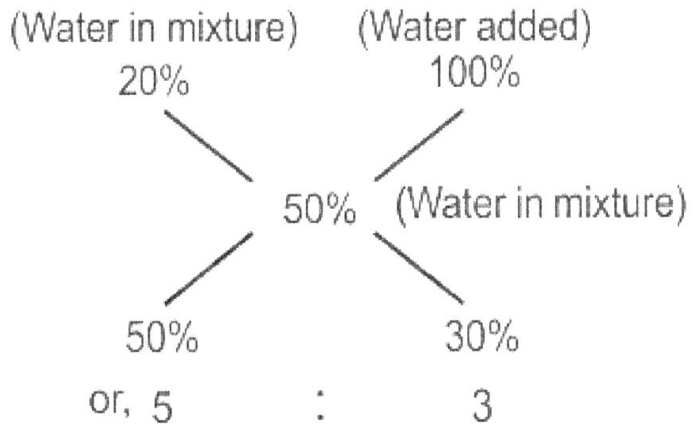

(Water in mixture) 20% (Water added) 100%

50% (Water in mixture)

50% 30%

or, 5 : 3

Percentage of water added = $\left(\frac{3}{8}\right) \times 100\% = 37.5\%$

∴ The percentage of water added is 37.5%.

17. A container has a capacity of 20 litres and is full of milk. 10 Litre of milk is taken out of it and replaced by the same quantity of water again 10 litres of mixture is taken out and replaced by an equal quantity of water. How much milk is left in the mixture?

A. 25 litres

B. 5 litres

C. 10 litres

D. 15 litres

Answer: B

Explanation:

Given:

A container has a capacity of 20 litres.

Here, the number of operations is 2, that is $n = 2$

Milk left in the container after n operations/Original quantity of milk in the container.

$= \left(\frac{(20-10)}{20}\right)^2 \times 20$

$= \left(\frac{10}{20}\right)^2 \times 20$

$\Rightarrow \frac{1}{4} \times 20 = 5$ litre

∴ 5 litre of milk is left in the mixture.

18. Copper and Zinc are in the ratio $1:4$ in 300gms of an alloy. The quantity (in grams) of copper to be added to it to make the ratio $4:3$ is:

A. 225gm

B. 250gm

C. 200gm

D. 260gm

Answer: D

Explanation:

Given:

In 300gms alloy ratio of copper and zinc $= 1:4$

Let the quantity of copper to be added be X.

The quantity of copper in 300gms alloy $= \left(\frac{1}{5}\right) \times 300$

$= 60$gm and the quantity of Zinc in 300gms alloy $= \left(\frac{4}{5}\right) \times 300 = 240$gm

According to the question,

$\Rightarrow \frac{(60+X)}{240} = \frac{4}{3}$

$\Rightarrow 60 + X = 320$

$\Rightarrow X = 320 - 60 = 260$gm

∴ The quantity of copper to be added is 260gm.

19. How many litres of water should be added to a 30 litre mixture of milk and water containing milk and water in the ratio of $7:3$ such that the resultant mixture has 40% water in it?

A. 2 litres

B. 5 litres

C. 6 litres

D. 9 litres

Answer: B

Explanation:

Given:

30 litres of the mixture has milk and water in the ratio $7:3$.

The solution has 21 litres of milk and 9 litres of water.

When you add more water, the amount of milk in the mixture remains constant at 21 litres.

In the first case, before addition of further water, 21 litres of milk accounts for 70% by the volume.

After water is added, the new mixture contains 60% milk and 40% water.

The 21 litres of milk accounts for 60% by volume.

100% volume $= \frac{21}{0.6} = 35$ litres

$\therefore$ 5 litres of water was added.

20. Type A chilli powder of Rs. 136 per kg and type B chilli powder of Rs. 168 per kg is mixed and the cost price of the mixture becomes Rs. 144 per kg. This mixture is 104 kg, if 14 kg of type A and 18 kg of type B was added into this mixture, what is the ratio of type A and type B mixture now?

A. $21:9$

B. $23:11$

C. $19:9$

D. $18:5$

Answer: B

Explanation:

Given:

Type A chilli powder = Rs. 136 per kg

Type B chilli powder = Rs. 168 per kg

Price of mixture = Rs. 144 per kg

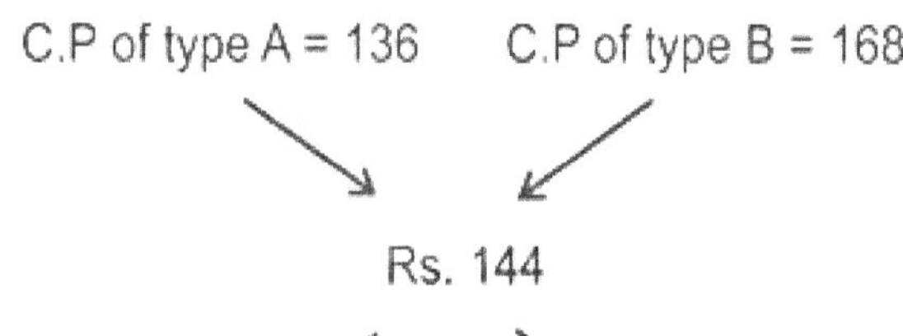

So, the ratio $= 24:8 = 3:1$

Total weight $= 104$ kg

Type $A = \frac{3}{4} \times 104 = 78$

Type $B = 104 - 78 = 26$

14 kg of type A is added $= 78 + 14 = 92$

18 kg of type B is added $= 26 + 18 = 44$

New ratio $= 92:44 = 23:11$

21. The ratio, in which tea costing Rs. 192 per kg is to be mixed with tea costing Rs. 150 per kg so that the mixed tea when sold for Rs. 194.40 per kg, gives a profit of 20%.
A. $2:5$
B. $3:5$
C. $5:3$
D. $5:2$

Answer: A
Explanation:
CP of first tea = Rs. 192 per kg.
CP of Second tea = Rs. 150 per kg.
The mixture is to be sold in Rs. 194.40 per kg, which has included 20% profit. So,
SP of Mixture = Rs. 194.40 per kg.
Let the CP of Mixture be Rs. X per kg. Therefore,
$X + 20\%$ of $X = SP$
$\frac{6X}{5} = 194.40$
$6X = 194.40 \times 5$
$X =$ Rs. 162 per kg.

Let N kg of first tea and M kg of second tea to be added.
Now, Using Alligation,
We get,

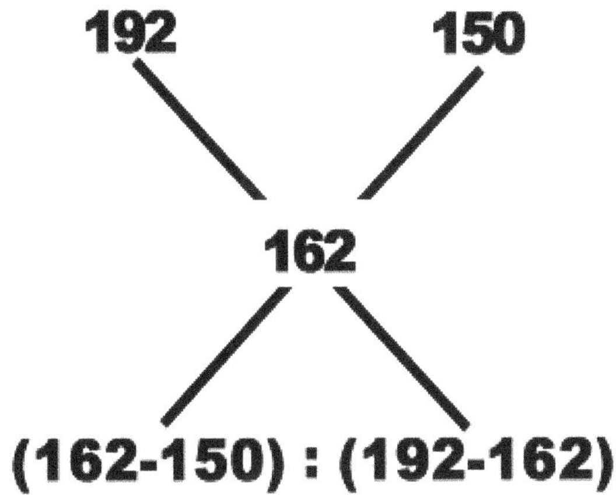

$\frac{N}{M} = \frac{12}{30}$
$N: M = 2: 5$

22. An alloy contains zinc, copper and tin in the ratio 2: 3: 1 and another contains copper, tin and lead in the ratio 5: 4: 3. If equal weights of both alloys are melted together to form a third alloy, then the weight of lead per kg in new alloy will be:
A. $\frac{1}{2}$ kg
B. $\frac{1}{8}$ kg
C. $\frac{3}{14}$ kg
D. $\frac{7}{9}$ kg
Answer: B
Explanation:
Ratio of Zinc, Copper and Tin is given as,

$$Z: C: T = 2: 3: 1$$

Now, let the first alloy be 12 kg (taken as 4 kg Zinc, 6 kg Copper and 2Kg Tin). Weight of second alloy = 12 kg as, C: T: L = 5: 4: 3. (Taken as 5 kg Copper, 4 kg Tin and 3Kg Lead.)
Alloys are mixed together to form a third alloy. Then the ratio of content in it,

$$Z: C: T: L = 4: (6 + 5): (2 + 4): 3$$

Weight of third alloy = 12 + 12 = 24Kg.
So, weight of the Lead = $\frac{3}{24} = \frac{1}{8}$ kg.

23. In a 729 litres mixture of milk and water, the ratio of milk to water is $7:2$. To get a new mixture containing milk and water in the ratio $7:3$, the amount of water to be added is:

A. 81 litres
B. 71 litres
C. 56 litres
D. 50 litres

Answer: A
Explanation:

Quantity of milk in 729 litre of mixture $= 7 \times \frac{729}{9} = 567$ litre

Quantity of water $= 729 - 567$
$= 162$ litres

Let x litre of water be added to become ratio $7:3$

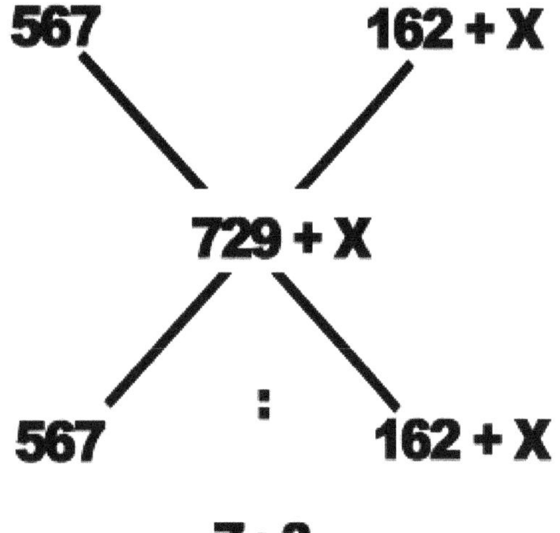

Or, $\frac{7}{3} = \frac{567}{162+x}$

Or, $162 \times 7 + 7x = 567 \times 3$

Or, $7x = 1701 - 1134 = 567$

Or, $x = \frac{567}{7} = 81$ litres water is to be added.

24. In what ratio must a mixture of 30% alcohol strength be mixed with that of 50% alcohol strength so as to get a mixture of 45% alcohol strength?

A. $1:2$
B. $1:3$
C. $2:1$

D. 3: 1

Answer: B
Explanation:

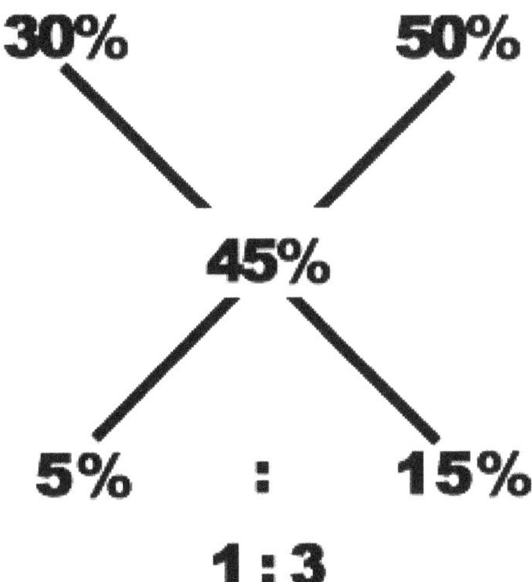

25. To gain 10% on selling sample of milk at the cost price of pure milk, the quantity of water to be mixed with 50 kg. of pure milk is:
A. 2.5 kg
B. 5 kg
C. 7.5 kg
D. 10 kg

Answer: B
Explanation:
1st Method (Method of Alligation):

Let the quantity of water to be mixed is x kg.

Let the cost of milk be Rs. 1 per kg.

Then SP of 50 kg of milk with gain 10% = Rs. 55 [As Cost of 50 kg milk = Rs. 50 , then SP = (50 + 10% of 50)]

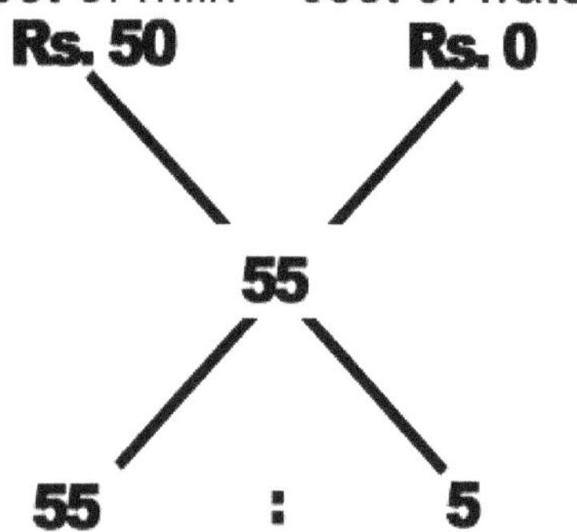

Then, water to be mixed is 5 kg, As the selling price of the milk is Rs. 1 per kg. Seller has to have 10% gain on 50 kg milk, he must have to add 5 kg water to 50 kg milk.

2nd Method (Simple Method):

Let the quantity of water mixed be xkg.

Let CP of 1 kg of pure milk = Rs. 1 .

Hence,

% gain $= x \times \frac{100}{50}$

$10 = \frac{100x}{50}$

Or, $2x = 10$

or, $x = 5$ kg.

26. From a container, full of pure milk, 20% is replaced by water and this process is repeated three times. At the end of third operation, the quantity of pure milk reduces to:

A. 40.0%
B. 50.0%
C. 51.2%
D. 58.8%

Answer: C
Explanation:
Let pure milk was 100 L. So,
Water is replaced 20% in per process = 20% of 100 = 20 L.
Now, we use short-cut formula for it.

Quantity of Milk reduced to,

$= X \times \left[1 - \frac{Y}{X}\right]^n$

$= 100 \times \left[1 - \frac{20}{100}\right]^3$

$= \frac{100 \times 64}{125}$

$= 51.2\%$

Here,

X = Initial quantity of milk.

Y = Replaced water in per process.

n = No. of process repeated

Note:

The formula used in above problem is quite similar to depreciation formula or Compound interest formula.

Alternatively,

Let pure milk be 100 litres initially.

After third operation, milk will be

$100 = 20\% \downarrow (-20\text{ L}) \Rightarrow 80 = 20\% \downarrow (-16\text{ L}) \Rightarrow 64 = 20\% \downarrow (-12.8 \Rightarrow 51.2\%$

27. Three types of wheat of Rs. 1.27, Rs. 1.29 and Rs. 1.32 per kg are mixed together to be sold at Rs. 1.30 per kg. In what ratio should this wheat be mixed?

A. 1: 2: 3

B. 2: 2: 3

C. 2: 3: 1

D. 1: 1: 2

Answer: D

Explanation:

Average cost: Rs. 1.30 per kg.

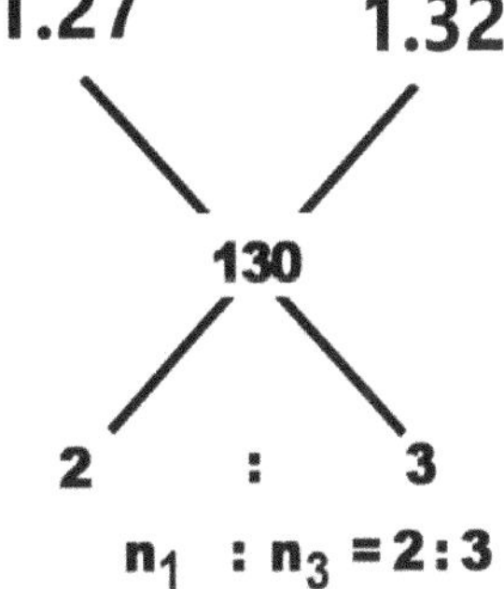

And

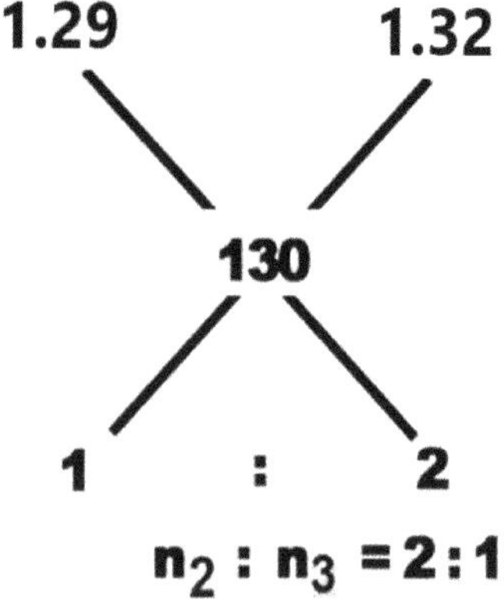

Hence, ratio of 1.27,1.29 and 1.32
$\Rightarrow n_1 : n_2 : n_3 = 2 : (2 \times 3) : 3$
$\Rightarrow n_1 : n_2 : n_3 = 2 : 6 : 3$

28. An amount of Rs. 680 was invested at 6% rate of interest and another sum of money was invested at 10% interest. If the average interest on the total at the end of the year was 7.5%, how much was invested at 10% ?

A. Rs. 408
B. Rs. 412.6
C. Rs. 267.5
D. None of these

Answer: A
Explanation:

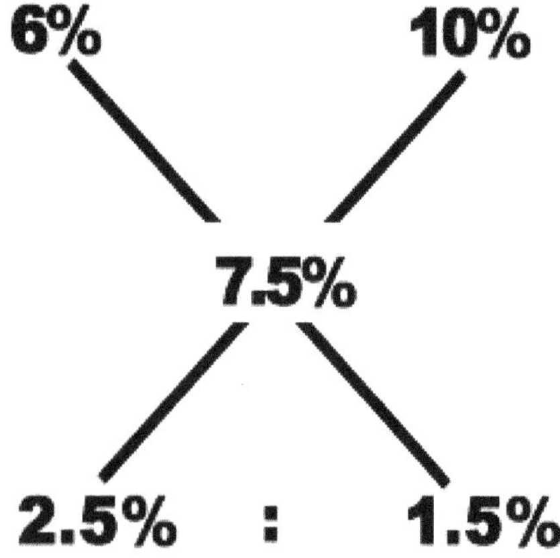

Now, $\frac{680}{x} = \frac{2.5}{1.5}$
Or, $x = \frac{680 \times 3}{5}$
Hence, $x =$ Rs. 408

29. A trader has 50 kg of pulses, part of which he sells at 14% profit and rest at 6% loss. On the whole his loss is 4%. How much quantity is sold at 14% profit and that at 6% loss?

A. 5 kg, 45 kg.

B. 15 kg, 35 kg.

C. 10 kg, 40 kg.

D. None of these

Answer: A

Explanation:

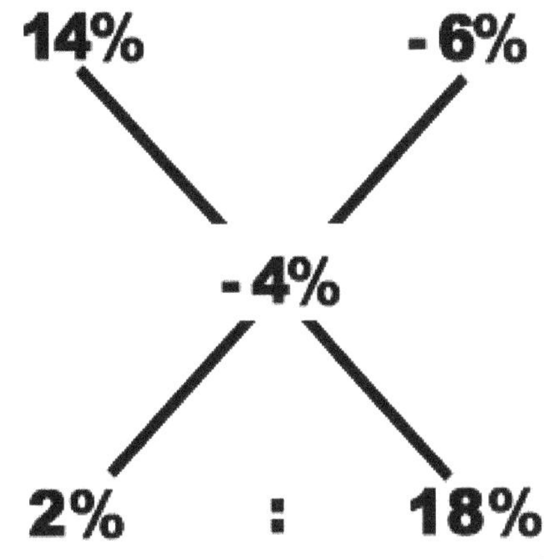

Hence, ratio of quantity sold at 14% profit and 6% loss,

$= 2{:}\,18 = 1{:}\,9$

Hence, pulses sold at 14% profit,

$= \frac{50 \times 1}{10} = 5$ kg

At 6% Wheat sold at loss = 45 kg.

30. Weights of two friends Ram and Shyam are in the ratio 4: 5. If Ram's weight is increased by 10% and total weight of Ram and Shyam become 82.8 kg, with an increases of 15%. By what percent did the weight of Shyam has to be increased?

A. 19%

B. 10%

C. 21%

D. 16%

Answer: A

Explanation:

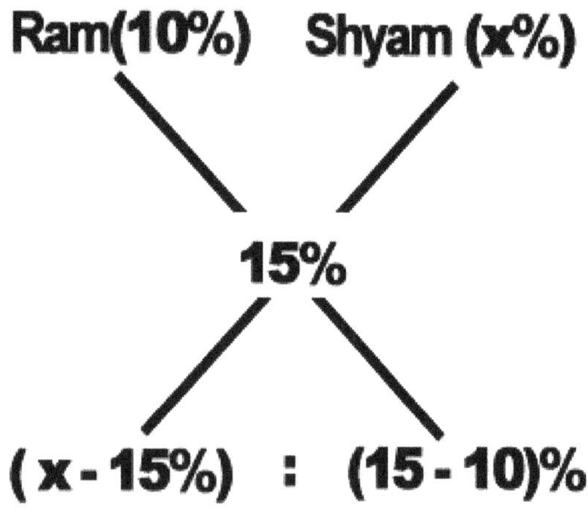

Now, given ratio of Ram and Shayam's weight = 4: 5

Hence, $\frac{x-15}{15-10}=\frac{4}{5}$

Or, $x=19\%$

31. A lump of two metals weighing 18 g is worth Rs. 87 but if their weight is interchanged, it would be worth Rs. 78.60. If the price of one metal be Rs. 6.70 per gram, find the weight of the other metal in the mixture.

A. 8 g
B. $12g$
C. 15 g
D. 18 g

Answer: A
Explanation:
Cost of (18 g of 1st metal +18 g of 2nd metal) = Rs. $165 \cdot 60$
Cost of (1 g of 1st metal +1 g metal of 2nd metal) = Rs. 9.20
Hence cost of 1 g of 2nd metal,
= 9.20 − 6.70
= Rs. 2.5
Mean price = Rs. $\frac{87}{18}$

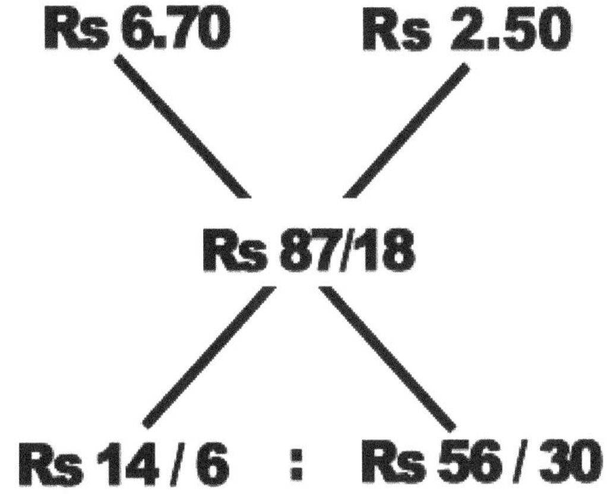

Now, $\frac{\text{quantity of 1}^{\text{st}}\text{ metal}}{\text{quantity of 2}^{\text{nd}}\text{ metal}} = \frac{14}{6} : \frac{56}{30} = 5:4$

Quantity of 2nd metal $= \frac{18 \times 4}{9} = 8$ g

32. A vessel contains milk and water in the ratio 3: 2. The volume of the contents is increased by 50% by adding water to it. From this resultant solution 30 L is withdrawn and then replaced with water. The resultant ratio of milk water in the final solution is 3: 7. Find the original volume of the solution.

A. 80 L
B. 65 L
C. 75 L
D. 82 L

Answer: A
Explanation:

Let the original volume be x. then, quantity of milk and water, $= \frac{3x}{5}$ and $\frac{2x}{5}$ respectively.

After adding water to it, the volume becomes 150%, the quantity of milk and water:

$= \frac{3x}{5}$ and $\frac{9x}{10}$

$$\frac{\frac{3x}{5} - 12}{\frac{9x}{10} + 12} = \frac{3}{7}$$

$14(3x - 60) = 3(9x + 120)$

Or, $x = 80$ L

33. 3 L water is taken out from vessel full of water and substituted by pure milk. This process is repeated two more times. Finally, the ratio of milk and water in the solution becomes 1728: 27. Find the volume of the original solution.

A. 3 L
B. 5 L
C. 4 L
D. 9 L

Answer: C
Explanation:
We use formula for it where
n = number of time process of out going repeated.
y = Out going milk in process.
x = Volume of original solution.
F = Final milk left in mixture.

$$F = x\left(1 - \frac{y}{x}\right)^n$$

Final quantity of water,

$$F = x\left(1 - \frac{3}{x}\right)^3$$

$$\frac{F}{x} = \left(\frac{x-3}{x}\right)^3$$

$$\frac{27}{1728} = \left(\frac{x-3}{x}\right)^3$$

$$\left(\frac{3}{12}\right)^3 = \left(\frac{x-3}{x}\right)^3$$

$$\frac{3}{12} = \frac{x-3}{x}$$

$x = 4$ L

34. One quantity of wheat at Rs 9.30 per Kg is mixed with another quality at a certain rate in the ratio 8: 7. If the mixture so formed be worth Rs10 per Kg, what is the rate per Kg of the second quality of wheat?
A. Rs. 12.47
B. Rs. 10.80
C. Rs. 15.17
D. Rs. 47.66

Answer: B
Explanation:
Let the rate of second quality be Rs. x per Kg.

C.P of 1Kg wheat of 1st kind = 930p
C.P of 1Kg wheat of 2nd kind = 100 × p
Mean price = 1000p
By rule of alligation we have required ratio 8: 7
930x / (Mean Price) × (1000) / (x – 10): 0.7
So we get required ratio, $(x - 10): 0.7 :: 8: 7$
⇒ x = 10.80 per Kg

35. A vessel is filled with liquid, 3 parts of which are water and 5 parts syrup. How much of the mixture must be drawn off and replaced with water so that the mixture may be half water and half syrup?

A. $\frac{1}{3}$
B. $\frac{1}{4}$
C. $\frac{1}{5}$
D. $\frac{1}{7}$

Answer: C
Explanation:
Suppose the vessel initially contains 8 litres of liquid.
Let x litres of this liquid be replaced with water.
Quantity of water in new mixture = $\left(3 - \frac{3x}{8} + x\right)$ litres
Quantity of syrup in new mixture = $\left(5 - \frac{5x}{8}\right)$ litres

$$\therefore 3 - \frac{3x}{8} + x = 5 - \frac{5x}{8}$$

$$\Rightarrow 5x + 24 = 40 - 5x$$

$$\Rightarrow 10x = 16$$

$$\Rightarrow x = \frac{8}{5}$$

So, part of the mixture replaced.

$$= \frac{8}{5} \times \frac{1}{8}$$

$$= \frac{1}{5}$$

36. Tea worth Rs. 126 per kg and Rs. 135 per kg are mixed with a third variety in the ratio 1: 1: 2. If the mixture is worth Rs. 153 per kg, the price of the third variety per kg will be:

A. Rs. 169.50
B. Rs. 170
C. Rs. 175.50
D. Rs. 180

Answer: C
Explanation:
Since the first and second varieties are mixed in equal proportions.
So, their average price
$= \text{Rs.} \left(\frac{126 + 135}{2}\right)$
$= \text{Rs. } 130.50$
So, the mixture is formed by mixing two varieties, one at Rs. 130.50 per kg and the other at say, Rs. x per kg in the ratio 2: 2, i.e., 1: 1. We have to find x.
By the rule of alligation, we have:

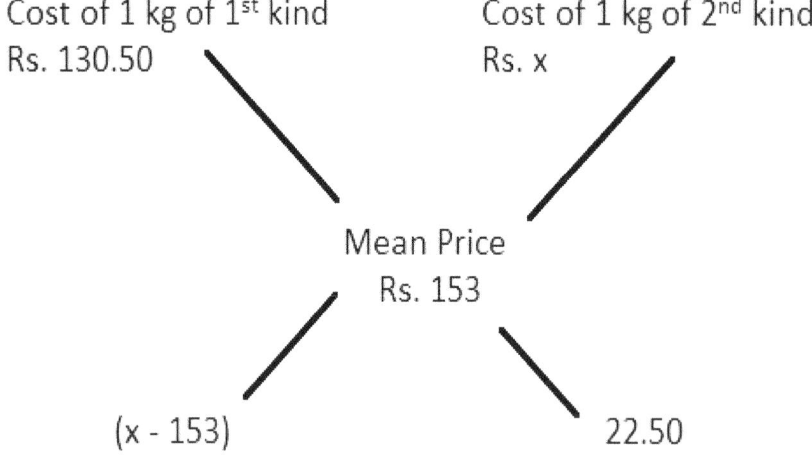

$\therefore \frac{x - 153}{22.50} = 1$
$\Rightarrow x - 153 = 22.50$
$\Rightarrow x = 175.50$

37. A can contains a mixture of two liquids A and B is the ratio 7: 5. When 9 litres of mixture are drawn off and the can is filled with B, the ratio of A and B becomes 7: 9. How many litres of liquid A was contained by the can initially?
A. 10
B. 20
C. 21
D. 25

Answer: C

Explanation:

Suppose the can initially contains

$7x$ and $5x$ of mixtures A and B respectively.

Quantity of A in mixture left

$= \left(7x - \frac{7}{12} \times 9\right)$ litres

$= \left(7x - \frac{21}{4}\right)$ litres

Quantity of B in mixture left

$= \left(5x - \frac{5}{12} \times 9\right)$ litres

$= \left(5x - \frac{15}{4}\right)$ litres

$$\therefore \frac{\left(7x - \frac{21}{4}\right)}{\left(5x - \frac{15}{4}\right) + 9} = \frac{7}{9}$$

$$\Rightarrow \frac{28x - 21}{20x + 21} = \frac{7}{9}$$

$\Rightarrow 252x - 189 = 140x + 147$

$\Rightarrow 112x = 336$

$\Rightarrow x = 3$

So, the can contained 21 litres of A

38. A milk vendor has 2 cans of milk. The first contains 25% water and the rest milk. The second contains 50% water. How much milk should he mix from each of the containers so as to get 12 litres of milk such that the ratio of water to milk is 3: 5 ?

A. 4 litres, 8 litres

B. 6 litres, 6 litres

C. 5 litres, 7 litres

D. 7 litres, 5 litres

Answer: B

Explanation:

Let the cost of 1 litre milk be Rs. 1

Milk in 1 litre mixture in 1st can = $\frac{3}{4}$ litre, C.P. of 1 litre mixture in 1st can Rs. $\frac{3}{4}$ Milk in 1 litre mixture in 2nd can = $\frac{1}{2}$ litre, C.P. of 1 litre mixture in 2nd can Rs. $\frac{1}{2}$ Milk in 1 litre of final mixture = $\frac{5}{8}$ litre, Mean price = Rs. $\frac{5}{8}$ By the rule of alligation, we have:

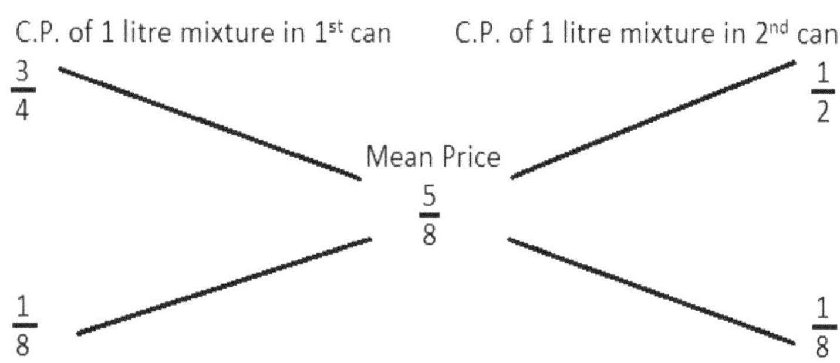

∴ Ratio of two mixtures = $\frac{1}{8}:\frac{1}{8} = 1:1$

So, quantity of mixture taken from each can = $\left(\frac{1}{2} \times 12\right)$ = 6 litres

39. In what ratio must a grocer mix two varieties of pulses costing Rs. 15 and Rs. 20 per kg respectively so as to get a mixture worth Rs. 16.50 kg ?

A. $3:7$

B. $5:7$

C. $7:3$

D. $7:5$

Answer: C

Explanation:

By the rule of alligation, we have:

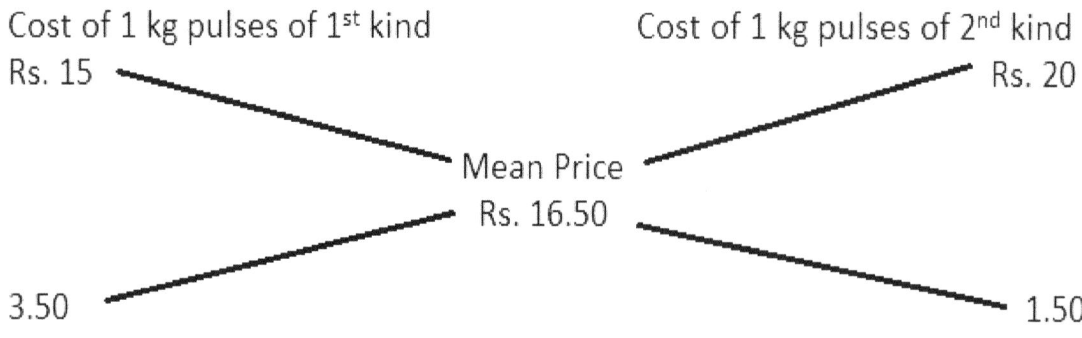

∴ Required rate = $3.50:1.50 = 7:3$

40. A dishonest milkman professes to sell his milk at cost price but he mixes it with water and thereby gains 25%. The percentage of water in the mixture is:

A. 4%
B. 16%
C. 20%
D. 25%

Answer: C
Explanation:
Let C.P. of 1 litre milk be Rs. 1
Then, S.P. of 1 litre of mixture = Rs. 1 , Gain = 25%
C.P. of 1 litre mixture = Rs. $\left(\frac{100}{125} \times 1\right) = \frac{4}{5}$
By the rule of alligation, we have:

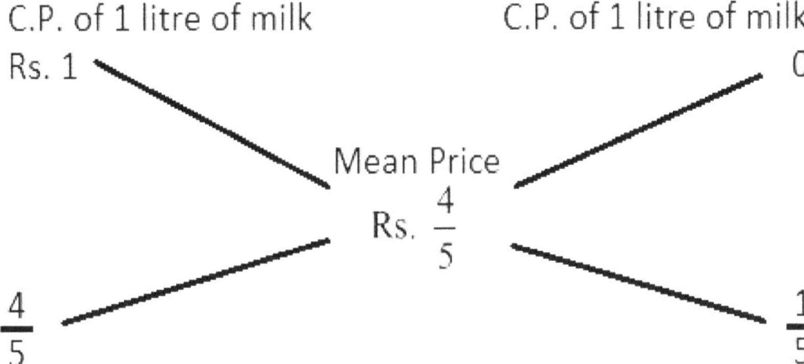

$\therefore$ Ratio of milk to water $= \frac{4}{5} : \frac{1}{5} = 4:1$
Hence, percentage of water in the mixture = $\left(\frac{1}{5} \times 100\right)\% = 20\%$

41. A container contains 40 litres of milk. From this container 4 litres of milk was taken out and replaced by water. This process was repeated further two times. How much milk is now contained by the container?

A. 26.34 litres
B. 27.36 litres
C. 28 litres
D. 29.16 litres

Answer: D
Explanation:
Amount of milk left after 3 operations = $\left[40\left(1 - \frac{4}{40}\right)^3\right]$ litres

$= \left(40 \times \frac{9}{10} \times \frac{9}{10} \times \frac{9}{10}\right)$ litres
= 29.16 litres

42. A jar full of whisky contains 40% alcohol. A part of this whisky is replaced by another containing 19% alcohol and now the percentage of alcohol was found to be 26%. The quantity of whisky replaced is:

A. $\frac{1}{3}$
B. $\frac{2}{3}$
C. $\frac{2}{5}$
D. $\frac{3}{5}$

Answer: B
Explanation:
By the rule of alligation, we have:

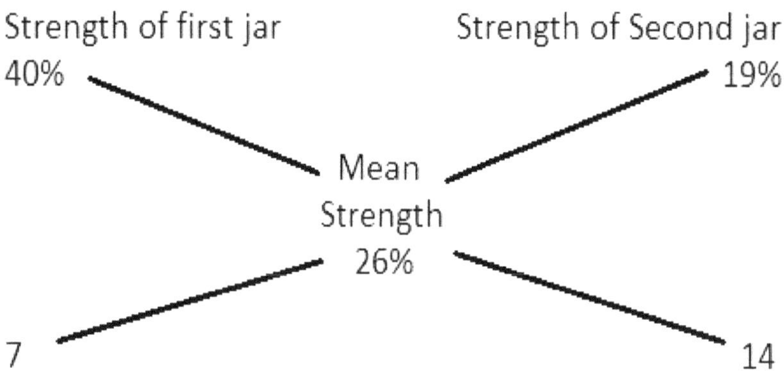

So, ratio of 1st and 2nd quantities = $7:14 = 1:2$
$\therefore$ Required quantity replaced $= \frac{2}{3}$

43. In what ratio must water be mixed with milk to gain $16\frac{2}{3}\%$ on selling the mixture at cost price?

A. $1:6$
B. $6:1$
C. $2:3$
D. $4:3$

Answer: A
Explanation:
Let C.P. of 1 litre milk be Rs. 1

S.P. of 1 litre of mixture = Rs. 1, Gain = $\frac{50}{3}\%$

$\therefore$ C.P. of 1 litre of mixture $= 100 \times \frac{3}{350} \times 1 = \frac{6}{7}$

BY the rule of alligation, we have:

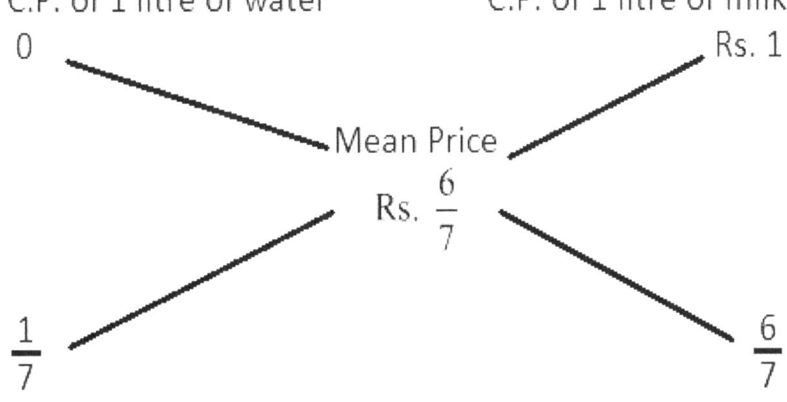

$\therefore$ Ration of water and milk $= \frac{1}{7} : \frac{6}{7} = 1:6$

44. Find the ratio in which rice at Rs. 7.20 a kg be mixed with rice at Rs. 5.70 a kg to produce a mixture worth Rs. 6.30akg.

A. 1:3

B. 2:3

C. 3:4

D. 4:5

Answer: B

Explanation:

By the rule of alligation:

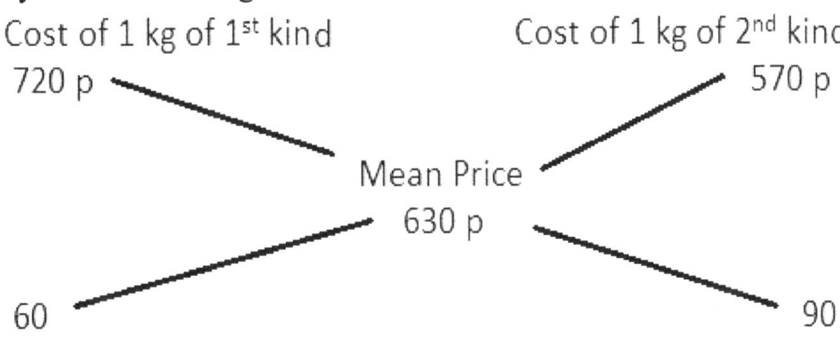

$\therefore$ Required ratio = 60: 90 = 2: 3

45. In what ratio must a grocer mix two varieties of tea worth Rs. 60 a kg and Rs. 65 a kg so that by selling the mixture at Rs. 68.20 a kg he may gain 10% ?

A. 3: 2

B. 3: 4

C. 3: 5
D. 4: 5

Answer: A
Explanation:
S.P. of 1 kg of the mixture $=$ Rs. 68.20, Gain $= 10\%$

C.P. of 1 kg of the mixture $=$ Rs. $\left(\frac{100}{110} \times 68.20\right) =$ Rs. 62

By the rule of alligation, we have:

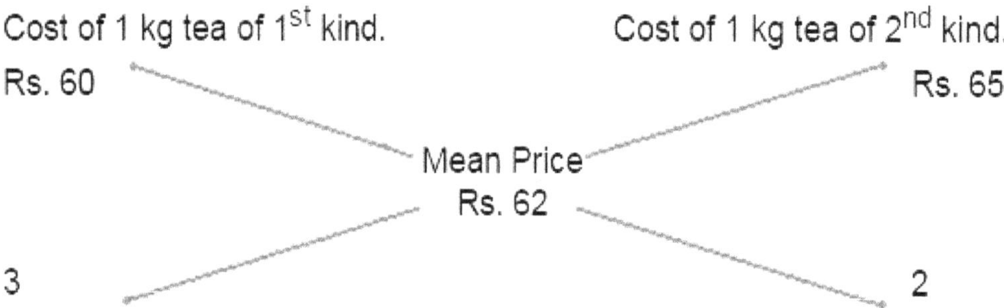

∴ Required ratio = 3: 2

46. The cost of Type 1 rice is Rs. 15 per kg and Type 2 rice is Rs. 20 per kg. If both Type 1 and Type 2 are mixed in the ratio of 2: 3, then the price per kg of the mixed variety of rice is:

A. Rs. 18
B. Rs. 18.50
C. Rs. 19
D. Rs. 19.50

Answer: A
Explanation:
Let the price of the mixed variety be Rs. x per kg.
By rule of alligation, we have:

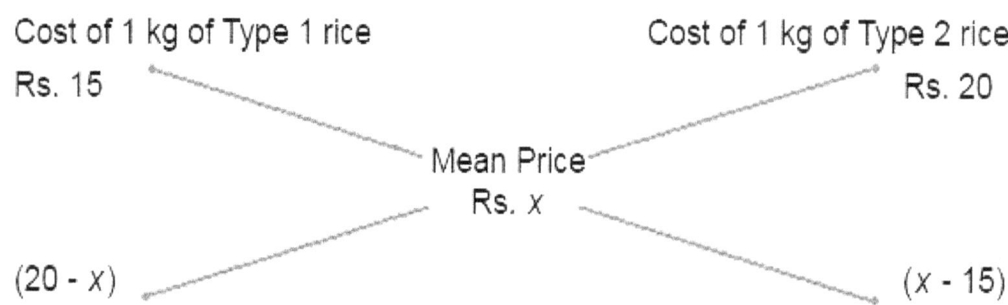

$$\therefore \frac{20 - x}{x - 15} = \frac{2}{3}$$
$$\Rightarrow 60 - 3x = 2x - 30$$
$$\Rightarrow 5x = 90$$
$$\Rightarrow x = 18$$

47. 8 litres are drawn from a cask full of wine and is then filled with water. This operation is performed three more times. The ratio of the quantity of wine now left in cask to that of water is 16: 65. How much wine did the cask hold originally?

A. 18 litres
B. 24 litres
C. 32 litres
D. 42 litres

Answer: B
Explanation:
Let the quantity of the wine in the cask originally be x litres.
Then, quantity of wine left in cask after 4 operations

$$= \left[x\left(1 - \frac{8}{x}\right)^4\right] \text{ litres}$$

$$\therefore \left(\frac{x\left(1 - \left(\frac{8}{x}\right)\right)^4}{x}\right) = \frac{16}{81}$$

$$\Rightarrow \left(1 - \frac{8}{x}\right)^4 = \left(\frac{2}{3}\right)^4$$

$$\Rightarrow \frac{x - 8}{x} = \frac{2}{3}$$

$$\Rightarrow 3x - 24 = 2x$$

$$\Rightarrow x = 24 \text{ litres}$$

48. A merchant has 1000 kg of sugar, part of which he sells at 8% profit and the rest at 18% profit. He gains 14% on the whole. The quantity sold at 18% profit is:

A. 400 kg
B. 560 kg
C. 600 kg
D. 640 kg

Answer: C

Explanation:

By the rule of alligation, we have:

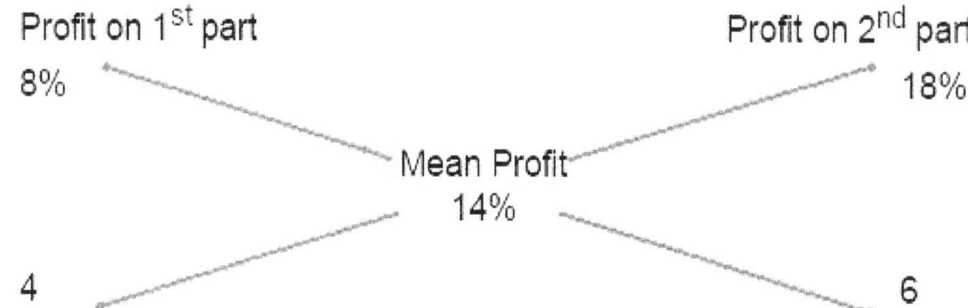

Ratio of 1st and 2nd parts

$= 4:6$

$= 2:3$

$\therefore$ Quantity of 2nd kind

$= \left(\frac{3}{5} \times 1000\right)$ kg

$= 600$ kg

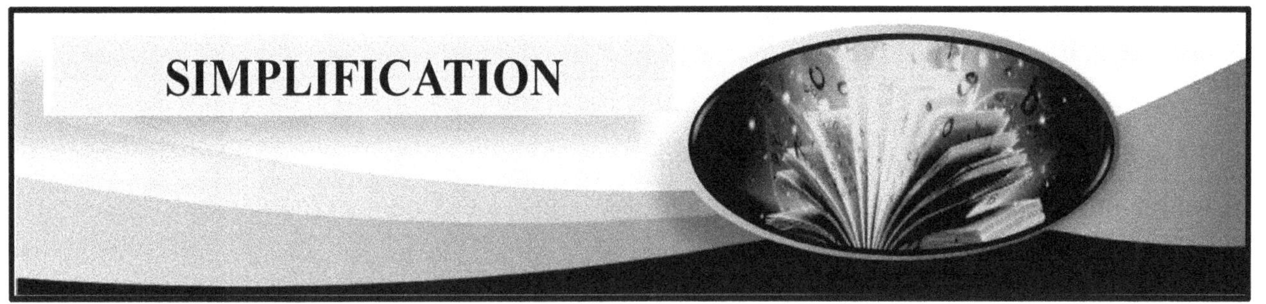

Introduction

Simplification refers to the process of reducing something to its most basic or essential form. It is a technique that is used in various fields such as mathematics, science, engineering, and communication to make complex concepts or ideas more understandable.

In mathematics, simplification involves reducing an expression to its simplest form by combining terms, factoring, or using other algebraic techniques. For example, the expression $3x + 6x$ can be simplified to $9x$ by combining the like terms.

In science, simplification involves reducing complex systems or processes to simpler ones, making them easier to understand and analyze. This can be done by breaking down a complex system into smaller components, identifying patterns or relationships, and eliminating unnecessary details.

In engineering, simplification involves designing products or processes that are simpler, more efficient, and cost-effective. This can be achieved by using simpler components, reducing the number of steps involved in a process, and minimizing waste or inefficiencies.

In communication, simplification involves conveying complex ideas or concepts in a clear and concise manner. This can be done by using simple language, avoiding jargon or technical terms, and using visual aids such as diagrams or charts to illustrate key points.

Overall, simplification is an important tool for making complex information more accessible and easier to understand. It allows us to break down complex concepts or systems into their most basic elements, making them more manageable and easier to work with.

Rule Of Simplification

The rule of simplification is a set of guidelines or principles that are used to simplify complex mathematical expressions or equations. These rules help to reduce the complexity of an expression or equation and make it easier to solve. Here are some common rules of simplification:

1. Use the distributive property: The distributive property states that $a(b + c) = ab + ac$. This property is useful for expanding and simplifying expressions that involve multiplication and addition.
2. Combine like terms: In an expression or equation, terms that have the same variables raised to the same power can be combined by adding or subtracting them.
3. Simplify fractions: Fractions can be simplified by dividing both the numerator and denominator by their greatest common factor.
4. Use the laws of exponents: The laws of exponents are rules that govern the way exponents interact with each other. For example, $x^a \times x^b = x^{(a+b)}$ and $(x^a)^b = x^{(ab)}$.
5. Use inverse operations: Inverse operations are operations that undo each other. For example, addition and subtraction are inverse operations, as are multiplication and division. By using inverse operations, you can isolate variables and solve them.
6. Use logarithms: Logarithms can be used to simplify expressions that involve exponents. For example, $\log(a \times b) = \log(a) + \log(b)$.

Formula Of Simplification

There is no single formula for simplification as it depends on the type of expression or equation being simplified. However, there are some common formulas or rules that are used in simplification. Here are some of them:

1. **Distributive Property:** $a(b + c) = ab + ac$. This formula is useful for expanding and simplifying expressions that involve multiplication and addition.

2. **Laws of Exponents:** The laws of exponents govern the way exponents interact with each other. Some common laws of exponents are:

- $x^a \times x^b = x^{(a+b)}$
- $(x^a)^b = x^{(ab)}$
- $x^{(a-b)} = 1/x^{(b-a)}$

3. **Laws of Logarithms:** Logarithms can be used to simplify expressions that involve exponents. Some common laws of logarithms are:

- $\log(a \times b) = \log(a) + \log(b)$
- $\log(a/b) = \log(a) - \log(b)$
- $\log(a^b) = b \times \log(a)$

4. **Quadratic Formula:** The quadratic formula is used to solve quadratic equations of the form $ax^2 + bx + c = 0$, where a, b, and c are constants. The formula is:

- $x = (-b \pm \text{sqrt}(b^2 - 4ac)) / 2a$

Terms Of Simplification

Memorize Multiplication tables: By memorizing multiplication tables up to 20, you can solve problems involving multiplication quickly.

Use BODMAS: BODMAS is a rule that stands for Brackets, Orders, Division, Multiplication, Addition, and Subtraction. It tells you about the order in which you should perform mathematical operations. Following this rule ensures that you arrive at the correct answer.

Approximation: Sometimes, instead of solving a problem exactly, it is easier to approximate the answer. For example, instead of calculating 17.68 x 23.41, you can round off the numbers to 18 x 23, which will give you a close enough answer.

Canceling common factors: Cancelling common factors is a technique used to simplify complex fractions. If a numerator and a denominator have a common factor, you can cancel it out to simplify the fraction.

Using shortcuts: There are many shortcuts and tricks that can be used to simplify complex problems. For example, to find the square of a number ending in 5, you can multiply the tens digit by the next higher number and append 25 to the end.

MULTIPLE CHOICE QUESTIONS

1. **Direction:** What value will come in place of the question mark (?) in the following question?

$17 \times ? \times 22 = 52^2 + 2906$

A. 15

B. 16

C. 14

D. 21

Answer: A

Explanation:

Given:

$17 \times ? \times 22 = 52^2 + 2906$

On solving we get,

$$374 \times ? = 2704 + 2906$$
$$374 \times ? = 5610$$
$$? = \frac{5610}{374}$$
$$? = 15$$

So,

$? = 15$

2. **Direction:** What value will come in place of the question mark (?) in the following question?

110% of 940 + ?% of 140 = 1118

A. 95

B. 70

C. 60

D. 100

Answer: C

Explanation:

Given:

110% of $940 + ?\%$ of $140 = 1118$

On solving we get,

$$? \% \text{ of } 140 = 1118 - 110 \times \frac{940}{100} = 1118 - 1034 = 84$$

$$? = 84 \times \frac{100}{140} = 60$$

So, $? = 60$

3. Direction: What value will come in place of the question mark (?) in the following question?

53 × 47 - 94 × 86 + 26 × 14 = ?

A. -5329

B. -5029

C. -5229

D. -5169

Answer: C

Explanation:

Given:

$53 \times 47 - 94 \times 86 + 26 \times 14$

On solving we get,

$$= (50 + 3) \times (50 - 3) - (90 + 4) \times (90 - 4) + (20 + 6) \times (20 - 6)$$
$$= (50^2 - 3^2) - (90^2 - 4^2) + (20^2 - 6^2)$$
$$= 2491 - 8084 + 364$$
$$= -5229$$

So, $? = -5229$

4. If $-12 \times (-3) + [20 \div (-4) - (-24) \div 8] - [16 \div (-2)] = (-28 \div 7) + x$, then the value of x is:

A. 29

B. 39

C. 46

D. 47

Answer: C

Explanation:

Given,

$$-12 \times (-3) + [20 \div (-4) - (-24) \div 8] - [16 \div (-2)] = (-28 \div 7) + x$$
$$\Rightarrow -12 \times -3 + [20 \div (-4) + 24 \div 8] - [16 \div (-2)] = (-4) + x$$
$$\Rightarrow 36 + [(-5) + 3] - [-8] = (-4) + x$$
$$\Rightarrow 36 + (-2) + 8 = (-4) + x$$
$$\Rightarrow x = 46$$

5. 140.75 × 0.01 is:

A. 140.75

B. 14000.75

C. 1.4075

D. 0.14075

Answer: C

Explanation:

Given:

Any number when multiplied with 1 , gives the same number as the result.

Here, 0.01 is actually $\frac{1}{100}$ so we first multiply the given number by 1 : $140.75 \times 1 = 140.75$

Now, since the result is to be divided by 100 , we shift the decimal two places to the left.

$140.75 \times 0.01 = 1.4075$

6. The value of 0.9 ÷ (0.3 × 0.3) is:

A. 0.01

B. 0.1

C. 1

D. 10

Answer: D

Explanation:

Given:

$$0.9 \div (0.3 \times 0.3)$$
$$= 0.9 \div (0.09)$$
$$= \frac{0.9}{0.09} = \frac{0.90}{0.09} = \frac{90}{9} = 10$$

The value of 0.9 ÷ (0.3 × 0.3) is 10.

7. What will come in place of the question mark '?' in the following question?

$(0.1 \times 0.004) + (0.02 \times 0.3) - (0.04 \times 0.03) = \ ?$

A. 0.0022

B. 0.0034

C. 0.0046

D. 0.0052

Answer: C

Explanation:

Given

$$(0.1 \times 0.004) + (0.02 \times 0.3) - (0.04 \times 0.03) = ?$$
$$\Rightarrow 0.0004 + 0.006 - 0.0012 = ?$$
$$\Rightarrow 0.0064 - 0.0012 = ?$$
$$\therefore ? = 0.0052$$

8. Simplify:

$$\sqrt{[4 + \sqrt{(44 + \sqrt{10000})}]}$$

A. 8

B. 4

C. 6

D. 16

Answer: B

Explanation:

Given

$$\sqrt{[4 + \sqrt{(44 + \sqrt{10000})}]}$$
$$= \sqrt{[4 + \sqrt{(44 + 100)}]}$$
$$= \sqrt{[4 + \sqrt{144}]}$$
$$= \sqrt{[4 + 12]}$$
$$= \sqrt{[16]}$$
$$= 4$$

9. 16% of $25 \times 88 + 20\%$ of $135 - 16 \times (18 - 5\%$ of $200) =?$

A. 224

B. 169

C. 507

D. 251

Answer: D

Explanation:

Given

$$16\% \text{ of } 25 \times 88 + 20\% \text{ of } 135 - 16 \times (18 - 5\% \text{ of } 200) =?$$

$$\Rightarrow 16\% \text{ of } 25 \times 88 + 20\% \text{ of } 135 - 16 \times (18 - 10) =?$$

$$\Rightarrow \left(\frac{16}{100}\right) \times 25 \times 88 + \left(\frac{20}{100}\right) \times 135 - 16 \times (18 - 10) =?$$

$$\Rightarrow 4 \times 88 + 27 - 16 \times 8 =?$$

$$\Rightarrow 352 + 27 - 128 =?$$

$$\Rightarrow 379 - 128 =?$$

$$\Rightarrow 251 =?$$

$\therefore$ The value of ? is 251

10. 28.56% of $91 + 44.44\%$ of $162 = 400\%$ of ?

A. 28.5

B. 24.5

C. 26.5

D. 29.5

Answer: B

Explanation:

Given

$14.28\% = \frac{1}{7}, 28.56\% = \frac{2}{7}$

$11.11\% = \frac{1}{9}, 44.44\% = \frac{4}{9}$

28.56% of 91 + 44.44% of 162 = 400% of ?

$\Rightarrow 91 \times \left(\frac{2}{7}\right) + 162 \times \left(\frac{4}{9}\right) = \left(\frac{400}{100}\right) \times ?$

$\Rightarrow 26 + 72 = 4 \times ?$

$\Rightarrow ? = \frac{98}{4} = 24.5$

∴ The value of ? is 24.5.

11. What will come in the place of question mark '?' in the following question? 60% of 80 ÷ 16 × 30% of 70 = ?

A. 60

B. 61

C. 62

D. 63

Answer: D

Explanation:

The given expression is,

60% of 80 ÷ 16 × 30% of 70 = ?

⇒ 48 ÷ 16 × 21 = ?

⇒ 3 × 21 = ?

⇒ ? = 63

∴ The value of ? is 63.

12. Select the correct answer of 4 + 4.44 + 4.04 + 44.4 + 444 = ?

A. 472.88

B. 495.22

C. 577.2

D. None of these

Answer: D

Explanation:

Given

4 + 4.44 + 4.04 + 44.4 + 444

Adding decimals first:

$0.44 + 0.04 + 0.4 = 0.88$

Now adding $4 + 4 + 4 + 44 + 444 = 500$

$\Rightarrow 500 + 0.88 = 500.88$

13. If $x = 5 + \sqrt{79 + \sqrt{11 - \sqrt{49}}}$, then find $2x + 3$.

A. 31

B. 41

C. 29

D. 37

Answer: A

Explanation:

Given:

$$x = 5 + \sqrt{79 + \sqrt{11 - \sqrt{49}}}$$

$$\Rightarrow x = 5 + \sqrt{79 + \sqrt{11 - 7}}$$

$$\Rightarrow x = 5 + \sqrt{79 + \sqrt{4}}$$

$$\Rightarrow x = 5 + \sqrt{79 + 2}$$

$$\Rightarrow x = 5 + \sqrt{81}$$

$$\Rightarrow x = 5 + 9$$

$$\Rightarrow x = 14$$

Now, $2x + 3$

$$\Rightarrow 2 \times 14 + 3$$

$$\Rightarrow 31$$

$\therefore$ The value of $2x + 3$ is 31 .

14. Find the value of '?' in the following equation.

$$3\frac{1}{2} + 2\frac{3}{4} + 1\frac{1}{4} + 5\frac{1}{2} = ?$$

A. $11\frac{1}{4}$

B. 13

C. $12\frac{1}{2}$

D. 12

Answer: B

Explanation:

Given:

$$3\frac{1}{2}+2\frac{3}{4}+1\frac{1}{4}+5\frac{1}{2}=?$$
$$\Rightarrow \frac{7}{2}+\frac{11}{4}+\frac{5}{4}+\frac{11}{2}=?$$
$$\Rightarrow \frac{7}{2}+\frac{11}{2}+\frac{11}{4}+\frac{5}{4}=?$$
$$\Rightarrow \frac{18}{2}+\frac{16}{4}=?$$
$$\Rightarrow 9+4=?$$
$$\Rightarrow ?=13$$

15. Find the value of:

(8.33% of 216 - 12.5% of 112) + (83.33% of 90 - 6.25% of 144)`

A. 70

B. 65

C. 75

D. 55

Answer: A

Explanation:

Given:

$$(8.33\% \text{ of } 216 - 12.5\% \text{ of } 112) + (83.33\% \text{ of } 90 - 6.25\% \text{ of } 144)$$
$$\Rightarrow \left[\left\{\left(\frac{1}{12}\right)\times 216\right\}-\left\{\left(\frac{1}{8}\right)\times 112\right\}\right]+\left[\left\{\left(\frac{5}{6}\right)\times 90\right\}-\left\{\left(\frac{1}{16}\right)\times 144\right\}\right]$$
$$\Rightarrow (18-14)+(75-9)$$
$$\Rightarrow 4+66$$
$$\Rightarrow 70$$

$\therefore$ The required value is 70.

16. Simplify $456 \div 24 \times \sqrt{36} - 95 + 36$

A. 55

B. 62

C. 65

D. 70

Answer: A

Explanation:

Given expression,

$$456 \div 24 \times \sqrt{36} - 95 + 36$$
$$\sqrt{36} = 6$$
$$= 456 \div 24 \times 6 - 95 + 36$$
$$= 19 \times 6 - 95 + 36$$
$$= 114 - 95 + 36$$
$$= 150 - 95 = 55$$

17. Find the value of (?) question mark.

$$\frac{?\times 25 \times 10}{60} + \frac{8 \times 15 \times 22}{30} = 98$$

A. $2\frac{1}{5}$

B. $2\frac{3}{5}$

C. $2\frac{4}{5}$

D. $2\frac{2}{5}$

Answer: D

Explanation:

$$\frac{?\times 25 \times 10}{60} + \frac{8 \times 15 \times 22}{30} = 98$$
$$\Rightarrow \frac{?\times 25}{6} + \frac{8 \times 22}{2} = 98$$
$$\Rightarrow \frac{?\times 25 + 3(176)}{6} = 98$$
$$\Rightarrow ?\times 25 + 528 = 588$$
$$\Rightarrow ?\times 25 = 60$$
$$\Rightarrow ? = \frac{60}{25} = \frac{12}{5}$$

$\therefore ? = 2\frac{2}{5}$

18. $\frac{[(8\times5)+(4\times7)+5]}{\left[\left(\frac{15}{3}\right)+(24-9)\right]} = ?$

A. 3.87

B. 4.67

C. 3.65

D. 4.21

Answer: C

Explanation:

$$\frac{[(8\times5)+(4\times7)+5]}{\left[\left(\frac{15}{3}\right)+(24-9)\right]}$$
$$= \frac{[40+28+5]}{[5+15]}$$
$$= \frac{73}{20}$$
$$= 3.65$$

19. Simplify $\frac{2\frac{3}{4}}{1\frac{5}{6}} \div \frac{7}{8} \times \left(\frac{1}{3}+\frac{1}{4}\right) + \frac{5}{7} \div \frac{3}{4} \text{ of } \frac{3}{7}$

A. $\frac{56}{77}$

B. $\frac{49}{80}$

C. $\frac{2}{3}$

D. $\frac{29}{9}$

Answer: D

Explanation:

Given,

$$\frac{2\frac{3}{4}}{1\frac{5}{6}} \div \frac{7}{8} \times \left(\frac{1}{3}+\frac{1}{4}\right) + \frac{5}{7} \div \frac{3}{4} \text{ of } \frac{3}{7}$$

$$= \frac{\left(\frac{11}{4}\right)}{\left(\frac{11}{6}\right)} \div \frac{7}{8} \times \left(\frac{1}{3} + \frac{1}{4}\right) + \frac{5}{7} \div \frac{3}{4} \text{ of } \frac{3}{7}$$

$$= \frac{3}{2} \div \frac{7}{8} \times \left(\frac{1}{3} + \frac{1}{4}\right) + \frac{5}{7} \div \frac{3}{4} \text{ of } \frac{3}{7}$$

$$= \frac{12}{7} \times \left(\frac{1}{3} + \frac{1}{4}\right) + \frac{5}{7} \div \frac{3}{4} \text{ of } \frac{3}{7}$$

$$= \left(\frac{12}{7}\right) \times \left(\frac{7}{12}\right) + \frac{5}{7} \div \frac{3}{4} \times \frac{3}{7}$$

$$= \left(\frac{12}{7}\right) \times \left(\frac{7}{12}\right) + \frac{\left(\frac{5}{7}\right)}{\left(\frac{9}{28}\right)}$$

$$= \left(\frac{12}{7}\right) \times \left(\frac{7}{12}\right) + \frac{20}{9}$$

$$= 1 + \frac{20}{9} = \frac{29}{9}$$

20. What will come at the place of x ?

$0.8 \div 12 + 0.75 \times 0.25 = x$

A. 0.1578

B. 0.1938

C. 0.2356

D. 0.2535

Answer: D

Explanation:

Given: $0.8 \div 12 + 0.75 \times 0.25 = x$

$x = 0.8 \div 12 + 0.75 \times 0.25$

$x = 0.066 + 0.75 \times 0.25$

$x = 0.066 + 0.1875$

$x = 0.2535$

21. The value of $\sqrt{80} + 3\sqrt{245} - \sqrt{125}$ is:

A. $20\sqrt{5}$

B. $9\sqrt{5}$

C. $25\sqrt{5}$

D. $15\sqrt{5}$

Answer: A

Explanation:

Given:

$$\sqrt{80} + 3\sqrt{245} - \sqrt{125}$$
$$= \sqrt{80} + 21\sqrt{5} - 5\sqrt{5}$$
$$= 4\sqrt{5} + 21\sqrt{5} - 5\sqrt{5}$$
$$= 20\sqrt{5}$$

22. $5\frac{3}{4} + x + 2\frac{1}{2} = 10\frac{1}{8}$ Find the value of x:

A. $2\frac{1}{4}$

B. $2\frac{7}{8}$

C. $1\frac{7}{8}$

D. $1\frac{7}{6}$

Answer: C

Explanation:

Given

$$5\frac{3}{4} + x + 2\frac{1}{2} = 10\frac{1}{8}$$
$$\Rightarrow 5\frac{3}{4} + x + 2\frac{1}{2} = 10\frac{1}{8}$$
$$\Rightarrow \frac{23}{4} + x + \frac{5}{2} = \frac{81}{8}$$
$$\Rightarrow \frac{33}{4} + x = \frac{81}{8}$$
$$\Rightarrow x = \frac{15}{8} = 1\frac{7}{8}$$

∴ The value of x is $1\frac{7}{8}$.

23. Find the value of $(999)^2$ - 22.

A. 998007

B. 995997

C. 996997

D. 997997

Answer: D

Explanation:

Given:

$(999)^2 - 2^2$

We know that,

$a^2 - b^2 = (a + b) \times (a - b)$

According to the formula used,

$$(999)^2 - 2^2$$
$$= (999 + 2) \times (999 - 2)$$
$$= (1001) \times (997)$$
$$= (1000 + 1) \times (997)$$
$$= (1000 \times 997) + (1 \times 997)$$
$$= 997000 + 997$$
$$= 997997$$

∴ The value of $(999)^2 - 2^2$ is 997997.

24. The value of $\frac{(253)^3+(247)^3}{25.3\times25.3-624.91+24.7\times24.7}$ is 50×10^k, where the value of k is:

A. 3

B. -3

C. 4

D. 2

Answer: A

Explanation:

Given,

$$\frac{(253)^3 + (247)^3}{25.3 \times 25.3 - 624.91 + 24.7 \times 24.7} = 50 \times 10^k$$

$$\Rightarrow \frac{100 \times (253 + 247)(253 \times 253 - 62491 + 247 \times 247)}{253 \times 253 - 62491 + 247 \times 247} = 50 \times 10^k$$

$\Rightarrow \quad 100 \times 500 = 50 \times 10^k$

$\Rightarrow \quad 50 \times 10^3 = 50 \times 10^k$

On comparing both sides,

$$10^k = 10^3$$
$$\Rightarrow k = 3$$

25. The value of $4 - \frac{5}{1+\frac{1}{3+\frac{1}{2+\frac{1}{4}}}}$ is:

A. $\frac{1}{8}$

B. $\frac{1}{64}$

C. $\frac{1}{16}$

D. $\frac{1}{32}$

Answer: A

Explanation:

$$\Rightarrow 4 - \frac{5}{1 + \frac{1}{3 + \frac{4}{9}}}$$

$$\Rightarrow 4 - \frac{5}{1 + \frac{1}{\frac{31}{9}}}$$

$$\Rightarrow 4 - \frac{5}{1 + \frac{9}{31}}$$

$$\Rightarrow 4 - \frac{5}{\frac{40}{31}}$$

$$\Rightarrow 4 - \frac{5 \times 31}{40}$$

$$\Rightarrow \frac{160 - 155}{40}$$

$$\Rightarrow \frac{5}{40}$$

$$\Rightarrow \frac{1}{8}$$

26. Simplify $16 - 2 \div 14 + 6 \times 2$

A. $27\frac{12}{14}$

B. $29\frac{5}{7}$

C. $26\frac{5}{7}$

D. $27\frac{5}{8}$

Answer: A

Explanation:

Given,

$16 - 2 \div 14 + 6 \times 2$

$= 16 - \frac{2}{14} + 12$

$= 28 - \frac{2}{14}$

$= 28 - \frac{2}{14}$

$= \frac{28 \times 14 - 2}{14}$

$= \frac{392 - 2}{14}$

$= \frac{390}{14}$

$= 27\frac{12}{14}$

27. Simplify $18 + 5 - 2 \times 50 \div 5$

A. 3

B. 7

C. 8

D. 9

Answer: A

Explanation:

Given,

$18 + 5 - 2 \times 50 \div 5$

Using the BODMAS rule to solve the above expression, we get.

$18 + 5 - 2 \times 10$

$= 18 + 5 - 20$

$= 23 - 20$

$= 3$

28. Direction: What will come in place of question mark (?) in the following que

$(37)^2 = ? + [(11\sqrt{3} + 5\sqrt{3}) \times (9\sqrt{3} + 11\sqrt{3})]$

A. 411

B. 415

C. 409

D. 406

Answer: C

Explanation:

$$\Rightarrow (37)^2 = ? + [(11\sqrt{3} + 5\sqrt{3}) \times (9\sqrt{3} + 11\sqrt{3})]$$
$$\Rightarrow 1369 - [16\sqrt{3} \times 20\sqrt{3}] = ?$$
$$\Rightarrow 1369 - 16 \times 20 \times 3 = ?$$
$$\Rightarrow ? = 1369 - 960$$
$$\Rightarrow ? = 409$$

29. $\frac{6}{5-\frac{5}{3}} \div \frac{4-\frac{2}{4-\frac{1}{2}}}{5-\frac{3}{2}} - \frac{2}{5} \text{ of } \left\{\frac{6}{9} + \frac{2}{3} \text{ of } \frac{1}{2}\right\} = ?$

A. $1\frac{1}{3}$

B. $2\frac{13}{49}$

C. $1\frac{7}{16}$

D. $2\frac{3}{5}$

Answer: C

Explanation:

Given expression,

$$\frac{6}{5-\frac{5}{3}} \div \frac{4-\frac{2}{4-\frac{1}{2}}}{5-\frac{3}{2}} - \frac{2}{5} \times \left\{\frac{6}{9} + \frac{2}{3} \times \frac{1}{2}\right\}$$

$$= \frac{6}{\left(\frac{10}{3}\right)} \div \frac{4-\frac{2}{\left(\frac{7}{2}\right)}}{\left(\frac{7}{2}\right)} - \frac{2}{5} \times \left\{\frac{6}{9} + \frac{1}{3}\right\}$$

$$= \frac{6 \times 3}{10} \div \frac{4 - \frac{2 \times 2}{7}}{\left(\frac{7}{2}\right)} - \frac{2}{5} \times 1$$

$$= \frac{9}{5} \div \frac{\left(4 - \frac{4}{7}\right)}{\left(\frac{7}{2}\right)} - \frac{2}{5}$$

$$= \frac{9}{5} \div \left(\frac{24}{7} \times \frac{2}{7}\right) - \frac{2}{5}$$

$$= \frac{9}{5} \times \frac{49}{48} - \frac{2}{5}$$

$$= \frac{147}{80} - \frac{2}{5}$$

$$= \frac{147 - 32}{80}$$

$$= \frac{115}{80}$$

$$= \frac{23}{16}$$

$$= 1\frac{7}{16}$$

30. Simplify the equation

$\frac{1}{2} + \frac{1}{4} + \frac{1}{8} + \frac{1}{a} + \frac{1}{6} = \frac{2}{6} + \frac{1}{3} + \frac{2}{3}$ and find the value of a:

A. $\frac{25}{24}$

B. $\frac{24}{7}$

C. 3

D. $\frac{7}{24}$

Answer: B

Explanation:

Given:

$$\frac{1}{2}+\frac{1}{4}+\frac{1}{8}+\frac{1}{a}+\frac{1}{6}=\frac{2}{6}+\frac{1}{3}+\frac{2}{3}$$

$$\Rightarrow \frac{1}{a}=\frac{2}{6}+\frac{1}{3}+\frac{2}{3}-\frac{1}{2}-\frac{1}{4}-\frac{1}{8}-\frac{1}{6}$$

$$\Rightarrow \frac{1}{a}=\frac{(8+8+16-12-6-3-4)}{24}$$

$$\Rightarrow \frac{1}{a}=\frac{7}{24}$$

$$\Rightarrow a=\frac{24}{7}$$

∴ The value of a is $\frac{24}{7}$.

31. Simplify the equation $\frac{(120\div 20\times y+31)}{(8^2-6\times 4+y^2)}=1$ and find the value of y:

A. 6

B. 3

C. 4

D. 2

Answer: B

Explanation:

Given:

$$\text{Equation} = \frac{(120\div 20\times y+31)}{(8^2-6\times 4+y^2)}=1$$

$$\Rightarrow \frac{(120\div 20\times y+31)}{(8^2-6\times 4+y^2)}=1$$

$$\Rightarrow (120\div 20\times y+31)=(8^2-6\times 4+y^2)$$

$$\Rightarrow 6y+31=(64-24+y^2)$$

$$\Rightarrow 6y=y^2+40-31$$

$$\Rightarrow y^2-6y+9=0$$

$$\Rightarrow y^2-3y-3y+9=0$$

$$\Rightarrow y(y-3)-3(y-3)=0$$

$$\Rightarrow (y-3)(y-3)=0$$

$$\Rightarrow y-3=0$$

$$\Rightarrow y=3$$

∴ The value of y is 3 .

32. The value of $3 \div \left[(8-5) \div \left\{(4-2) + \left(2 + \frac{8}{13}\right)\right\}\right]$ is:

A. $\frac{15}{17}$

B. $\frac{13}{17}$

C. $\frac{15}{19}$

D. $\frac{13}{19}$

Answer: B

Explanation:

$$3 \div \left[(8-5) \div \left\{(4-2) \div \left(2 + \frac{8}{13}\right)\right\}\right]$$

$$= 3 \div \left[3 \div \left\{2 \div \frac{34}{13}\right\}\right]$$

$$= 3 \div \left[3 \div \frac{13}{17}\right] = 3 \div \frac{3 \times 17}{13}$$

$$= 3 \times \frac{13}{3 \times 17} = \frac{13}{17}$$

33. Find the value of – $\frac{\sqrt[4]{0.0625} + \sqrt[3]{0.008} + \sqrt{0.09} - 1}{\sqrt[3]{62.5 \times \sqrt[5]{32}}}$

A. 1.25

B. 2.40

C. 2.50

D. 0

Answer: D

Explanation:

Given-

$$\frac{\sqrt[4]{0.0625}+\sqrt[3]{0.008}+\sqrt{0.09}-1}{\sqrt[3]{62.5\times\sqrt[5]{32}}}$$

$$=\frac{\sqrt[4]{\frac{625}{10000}}+\sqrt[3]{\frac{8}{1000}}+\sqrt{\frac{9}{100}}-1}{\sqrt[3]{62.5\times\sqrt[5]{2^5}}}$$

$$=\frac{\sqrt[4]{\frac{5^4}{10^4}}+\sqrt[3]{\frac{2^3}{10^3}}+\sqrt{\frac{3^2}{10^2}}-1}{\sqrt[3]{62.5\times 2}}$$

$$=\frac{\frac{5}{10}+\frac{2}{10}+\frac{3}{10}-1}{\sqrt[3]{125}}$$

$$=\frac{\frac{10}{10}-1}{5}$$

$$=\frac{1-1}{5}$$

$$=0$$

34. The expression $\frac{15(\sqrt{10}+\sqrt{5})}{\sqrt{10}+\sqrt{20}+\sqrt{40}-\sqrt{5}-\sqrt{80}}$ is equal to:

A. $[5(3+2\sqrt{2})]$

B. $5-2\sqrt{5}$

C. $5+2\sqrt{2}$

D. $10(3+2\sqrt{5})$

Answer: A

Explanation:

Given:

$$[15(\sqrt{10}+\sqrt{5})]\div[(\sqrt{10}+\sqrt{20}+\sqrt{40}-\sqrt{5}-\sqrt{80})]$$

$$=[15\times\sqrt{5}(\sqrt{2}+\sqrt{1})]\div[\sqrt{5}\times(\sqrt{2}+\sqrt{4}+\sqrt{8}-1-\sqrt{16})]$$

$$=[15\times(\sqrt{2}+\sqrt{1})]\div[(\sqrt{2}+2+\sqrt{8}-1-4)]$$

$$=[15\times(\sqrt{2}+\sqrt{1})]\div[\sqrt{2}(1+2)-3]$$

$$=[15\times(\sqrt{2}+\sqrt{1})]\div[3\sqrt{2}-3]$$

$$=[15\times(\sqrt{2}+\sqrt{1})]\div[3(\sqrt{2}-1)]$$

$$=[5\times(\sqrt{2}+\sqrt{1})]\div[(\sqrt{2}-1)]$$

By using rationalization,

$$= \frac{[5(\sqrt{2} + \sqrt{1})]}{[(\sqrt{2} - 1)]} \times \frac{(\sqrt{2} + 1)}{(\sqrt{2} + 1)}$$

$$= \frac{\left[5(\sqrt{2} + \sqrt{1})^2\right]}{[(\sqrt{2} - 1)(\sqrt{2} + 1)]}$$

$$= [5(2 + 1 + 2\sqrt{2})]$$

$$= [5(3 + 2\sqrt{2})]$$

$\therefore$ The simplified value is $[5(3 + 2\sqrt{2})]$.

35. Let $x = \left(\frac{\sqrt{1875}}{\sqrt{3888}} \div \frac{\sqrt{1200}}{\sqrt{768}}\right) \times \frac{\sqrt{175}}{\sqrt{1792}}$. Then $\sqrt{x}$ is equal to:

A. $\frac{4}{9}$

B. $\frac{5}{9}$

C. $\frac{5}{12}$

D. $\frac{7}{12}$

Answer: C

Explanation:

Given:

$$x = \left(\frac{\sqrt{1875}}{\sqrt{3888}} \div \frac{\sqrt{1200}}{\sqrt{768}}\right) \times \frac{\sqrt{175}}{\sqrt{1792}}$$

$\Rightarrow \sqrt{1875} = \sqrt{(625 \times 3)}$

$= 25\sqrt{3}$

$\Rightarrow \sqrt{3888} = \sqrt{(1296 \times 3)}$

$= 36\sqrt{3}$

$\Rightarrow \sqrt{1200} = \sqrt{(400 \times 3)}$

$= 20\sqrt{3}$

$\Rightarrow \sqrt{768} = \sqrt{(256 \times 3)}$

$= 16\sqrt{3}$

$\Rightarrow \sqrt{175} = \sqrt{(25 \times 7)}$

$= 5\sqrt{7}$

$\Rightarrow \sqrt{1792} = \sqrt{(256 \times 7)}$

$= 16\sqrt{7}$

$\Rightarrow x = \left[\left(\frac{25\sqrt{3}}{36\sqrt{3}}\right) \div \left(\frac{20\sqrt{3}}{16\sqrt{3}}\right)\right] \times \left(\frac{5\sqrt{7}}{16\sqrt{7}}\right)$

$\Rightarrow x = \left(\frac{25}{36}\right) \times \left(\frac{16}{20}\right) \times \left(\frac{5}{16}\right)$

$\Rightarrow x = \left(\frac{25}{(36 \times 4)}\right)$

$\Rightarrow \sqrt{x} = \sqrt{\left(\frac{25}{(36 \times 4)}\right)}$

$\Rightarrow \sqrt{x} = \left(\frac{5}{12}\right)$

$\therefore \sqrt{x}$ is $\left(\frac{5}{12}\right)$.

36. The value of $\frac{0.0203 \times 2.92}{0.7 \times 0.0365 \times 2.9} \div \frac{(12.12)^2 - (8.12)^2}{(0.25)^2 + (0.25)(19.99)}$ is:

A. 0.05

B. 0.01

C. 0.1

D. 0.5

Answer: A

Explanation:

Given:

$$\frac{0.0203 \times 2.92}{0.7 \times 0.0365 \times 2.9} \div \frac{(12.12)^2 - (8.12)^2}{(0.25)^2 + (0.25)(19.99)}$$

Using the BODMAS rule to solve the above expression, we get Let $\frac{0.0203 \times 2.92}{0.7 \times 0.0365 \times 2.9}$ be a' and $\frac{(12.12)^2 - (8.12)^2}{(0.25)^2 + (0.25)(19.99)}$ be b'

$\Rightarrow a \div b \ldots$ (i)

$$\Rightarrow a = \frac{0.0203 \times 2.92}{0.7 \times 0.0365 \times 2.9}$$

$$\Rightarrow a = \frac{203 \times 292 \times \frac{1}{10^6}}{7 \times 365 \times 29 \frac{1}{10^6}}$$

$$\Rightarrow a = \frac{292}{365} = 0.8 \ldots \text{(ii)}$$

$$\Rightarrow b = \frac{(12.12)^2 - (8.12)^2}{(0.25)^2 + (0.25)(19.99)}$$

$$\Rightarrow b = \frac{(12.12 + 8.12)(12.12 - 8.12)}{(0.25)^2 + (0.25)(19.99)}$$

$$\Rightarrow b = \frac{(20.24)(4)}{(0.25)^2 + (0.25)(19.99)}$$

$$\Rightarrow b = \frac{(20.24)(4)}{(0.25)(0.25 + 19.99)}$$

$$\Rightarrow b = \frac{(20.24)(4)}{(0.25)(20.24)}$$

$$\Rightarrow b = \frac{4}{0.25} = 16 \ldots\ldots \text{(iii)}$$

Put the value of a and b from eq. (ii) and (iii) to (i)

$$\Rightarrow a \div b = \frac{0.8}{16}$$

$= 0.05$

∴ The correct answer is 0.05 .

37. Simplify if,

$I = \frac{3}{5} \div \frac{5}{6}$

$II = 3 \div [(4 \div 5) \div 6]$

$III = [3 \div (4 \div 5)] \div 6$

$IV = 3 \div 4(5 \div 6)$

then,

A. I and II are equal.

B. III and IV are equal.
C. I and IV are equal.
D. II and III are equal.

Answer: B
Explanation:
According to question,

$$I = \frac{3}{5} \div \frac{5}{6}$$

$$I = \frac{3}{5} \times \frac{6}{5} = \frac{18}{25}$$

$$II = 3 \div \left[\frac{4}{5} \times \frac{1}{6}\right]$$

$$II = 3 \times \frac{30}{4}$$

$$II = \frac{45}{2}$$

$$III = [3 \div (4 \div 5)] \div 6$$

$$III = \left[3 \times \frac{5}{4}\right] \times \frac{1}{6}$$

$$III = \frac{5}{8}$$

$$IV = 3 \div 4(5 \div 6)$$

$$IV = 3 \div 4 \times \frac{5}{6}$$

$$IV = \frac{3}{4} \times \frac{5}{6}$$

$$IV = \frac{5}{8}$$

$\therefore$ III and IV are equal.

38. Simplify:

$3.\overline{87} - 2 \cdot \overline{59} = ?$

A. 1.20

B. $1.\overline{2}$

C. $1.\overline{27}$

D. $1.\overline{28}$

Answer: D

Explanation:

$$3.\overline{87} - 2.\overline{59} = (3 + 0.\overline{87}) - (2 + 0.\overline{59})$$

$$= \left(3 + \frac{87}{99}\right) - \left(2 + \frac{59}{99}\right)$$

$$= 1 + \left(\frac{87}{99} - \frac{59}{99}\right)$$

$$= 1 + \frac{28}{99}$$

$$= 1.\overline{28}$$

39. Find the value of $999\frac{1}{7} + 999\frac{2}{7} + 999\frac{3}{7} + 999\frac{4}{7} + 999\frac{5}{7} + 999\frac{6}{7}$:

A. 5997

B. 5979

C. 5994

D. 6997

Answer: A

Explanation:

$$999\frac{1}{7} + 999\frac{2}{7} + 999\frac{3}{7} + 999\frac{4}{7} + 999\frac{5}{7} + 999\frac{6}{7}$$

$$= 999 + \frac{1}{7} + 999 + \frac{2}{7} + 999 + \frac{3}{7} + 999 + \frac{4}{7} + 999 + \frac{5}{7} + 999 + \frac{6}{7}$$

$$6 \times 999 + \frac{1 + 2 + 3 + 4 + 5 + 6}{7} = 5994 + 3 = 5997$$

40. $\frac{6.75\times6.75\times6.75-4.25\times4.25\times4.25}{67.5\times67.5+42.5\times42.5+67.5\times42.5} =?$

A. 2.5

B. 0.25

C. 0.0025

D. 0.025

Answer: D

Explanation:

Identity used:

$a^3 - b^3 = (a - b)(a^2 + b^2 + ab)$

$$\Rightarrow \frac{6.75 \times 6.75 \times 6.75 - 4.25 \times 4.25 \times 4.25}{67.5 \times 67.5 + 42.5 \times 42.5 + 67.5 \times 42.5}$$

$$\Rightarrow \frac{[(6.75 - 4.25)(6.75 \times 6.75 + 4.25 \times 4.25 + 6.75 \times 4.25)]}{[100 \times (6.75 \times 6.75 + 4.25 \times 4.25 + 6.75 \times 4.25)}$$

$\Rightarrow ? = 2.5/100$

$\Rightarrow ? = 0.025$

$\therefore ? = 0.025$

41. Find the value of:

$$\frac{(0.0112 - 0.0012) \text{ of } 0.14 + 0.25 \times 0.2}{0.02 \times 0.01}$$

A. 257

B. 25.7

C. 2.57

D. 0.0257

Answer: A

Explanation:

Given :

$$\frac{(0.0112 - 0.0012) \text{ of } 0.14 + 0.25 \times 0.2}{0.02 \times 0.01}$$

$$= \frac{(0.01) \text{ of } 0.14 + 0.05}{0.0002}$$

$$= \frac{0.01 \times 0.14 + 0.05}{0.0002}$$

$$= \frac{0.0014 + 0.05}{0.0002}$$

$$= \frac{0.0514}{0.0002}$$

$= 257$

42. What should come in the place of question mark (?) in the following question?

$$\frac{7.2}{\sqrt[3]{0.729}} = \frac{(?)^3}{(2)^3}$$

A. 4

B. 5

C. 6

D. 8

Answer: A

Explanation:

Given,

$$\frac{7.2}{\sqrt[3]{0.729}} = \frac{(?)^3}{(2)^3}$$

$$\Rightarrow \frac{7.2}{\sqrt[3]{\frac{729}{1000}}} = \frac{(?)^3}{(2)^3}$$

$$\Rightarrow \frac{7.2}{\sqrt[3]{\left(\frac{9}{(10)}\right)^3}} = \frac{(?)^3}{(2)^3}$$

$$\Rightarrow \frac{7.2}{\sqrt[3]{(0.9)^3}} = \frac{(?)^3}{(2)^3}$$

$$\Rightarrow \frac{7.2}{0.9} = \frac{(?)^3}{(2)^3}$$

$$\Rightarrow 8 = \frac{(?)^3}{(2)^3}$$

$$\Rightarrow (2)^3 = \frac{(?)^3}{(2)^3}$$

$$\Rightarrow 2^3 \times 2^3 = (?)^3$$

$$\Rightarrow 4^3 = (?)^3$$

$$\Rightarrow ? = 4$$

$\therefore$ The value of ? is 4 .

43. Simplify : $1+\frac{2}{1+\frac{3}{1+\frac{4}{5}}}$

A. $\frac{7}{4}$

B. $\frac{4}{7}$

C. $\frac{7}{5}$

D. $\frac{3}{7}$

Answer: A

Explanation:

$$1+\frac{2}{1+\frac{3}{1+\frac{4}{5}}}$$

$$=1+\frac{2}{1+\frac{3}{9}}$$

$$=1+\frac{2}{1+\frac{5}{3}}$$

$$=1+\frac{2}{\frac{8}{3}}$$

$$=1+\frac{3}{4}$$

$$=\frac{7}{4}$$

44. Evaluate : $\frac{9|3-5|-5|4|\div 10}{-3(5)-2\times 4\div 2}$

A. $\frac{9}{10}$

B. $-\frac{8}{17}$

C. $-\frac{16}{19}$

D. $\frac{4}{7}$

Answer: C

Explanation:

According to question:

$$\frac{9|3-5|-5|4|\div 10}{-3(5)-2\times 4\div 2}$$

$$\Rightarrow \frac{9\times 2-20\div 10}{-15-2\times 2}$$

$$\Rightarrow \frac{18-2}{-15-4}$$

$$\Rightarrow -\frac{16}{19}$$

45. $5-[4-\{3-(3-3-6)\}]$ is equal to:

A. 10

B. 6

C. 4

D. 0

Answer: A

Explanation:

Given,

$$5-[4-\{3-(3-3-6)\}]$$
$$=5-[4-\{3-(-6)\}]$$
$$=5-[4-\{3+6\}]$$
$$=5-[4-\{9\}]$$
$$=5-[4-9]$$
$$=5-[-5]$$
$$=5+5$$
$$=10$$

46. Evaluate: $\frac{-(4-6)^2-3(-2)+|-6|}{18-9\div 3\times 5}$

A. $\frac{3}{8}$

B. $\frac{4}{7}$

C. $\frac{8}{3}$

D. $\frac{7}{4}$

Answer: C

Explanation:

$$\frac{-(4-6)^2 - 3(-2) + |-6|}{18 - 9 \div 3 \times 5}$$
$$= \frac{-(-2)^2 - (-6) + 6}{18 - 3 \times 5}$$
$$= \frac{-4 + 6 + 6}{18 - 15}$$
$$= \frac{8}{3}$$

47. What is the value of $36 \div 8 \times 4 + 2 \div 4 - 1 + 5$ of $3 \div (4 \times 2 - 3) - 3$?

A. $\frac{31}{2}$

B. 18

C. $\frac{35}{2}$

D. 16

Answer: C

Explanation:

$36 \div 8 \times 4 + 2 \div 4 - 1 + 5$ of $3 \div (4 \times 2 - 3) - 3$

Using BODMAS,

$\Rightarrow 36 \div 8 \times 4 + 2 \div 4 - 1 + 5$ of $3 \div (5) - 3$

$\Rightarrow 36 \div 8 \times 4 + 2 \div 4 - 1 + 15 \div (5) - 3$

$\Rightarrow 36 \div 8 \times 4 + 2 \div 4 - 1 + 3 - 3$

$$\Rightarrow \frac{36}{8} \times 4 + \frac{2}{4} - 1 + 3 - 3$$
$$\Rightarrow 18 + \frac{1}{2} - 1 + 3 - 3$$
$$\Rightarrow \frac{35}{2}$$

48. The value of $8 - [8 - (5 + 8) - \{8 - (8 - 5 + 8)\} + 10]$ is:

A. 5

B. 0

C. 20

D. 10

Answer: B

Explanation:

Consider 8 – [8 – (5 + 8) – {8 – (8 – 5 + 8)} + 10]

Using BODMAS rule:

= 8 – [8 – (5 + 8) – {8 – (11)} + 10]

= 8 – [8 – (5 + 8) – {-3} + 10]

= 8 – [8 – 13 + 3 + 10]

= 8 – [8]

= 0

49. The value of $6\frac{2}{3} + 2\frac{1}{2} \times 3\frac{3}{4} - 5\frac{1}{2} \times 4\frac{1}{4} + 1\frac{2}{3}\left(\frac{7}{8} + \frac{3}{4} \times \frac{2}{3}\right)$ is:

A. $-11\frac{1}{12}$

B. $11\frac{1}{12}$

C. $-5\frac{1}{24}$

D. $-6\frac{1}{2}$

Answer: C

Explanation:

Given,

$$\left(\frac{20}{3}\right) + \left(\frac{5}{2}\right) \times \left(\frac{15}{4}\right) - \left(\frac{11}{2}\right) \times \left(\frac{17}{4}\right) + \left(\frac{5}{3}\right)\left(\frac{7}{8} + \frac{3}{4} \times \frac{2}{3}\right)$$

$$= \left(\frac{20}{3}\right) + \left(\frac{5}{2}\right) \times \left(\frac{15}{4}\right) - \left(\frac{11}{2}\right) \times \left(\frac{17}{4}\right) + \left(\frac{5}{3}\right)\left(\frac{7}{8} + \frac{1}{2}\right)$$

$$= \left(\frac{20}{3}\right) + \left(\frac{5}{2}\right) \times \left(\frac{15}{4}\right) - \left(\frac{11}{2}\right) \times \left(\frac{17}{4}\right) + \left(\frac{5}{3}\right)\left(\frac{11}{8}\right)$$

$$= \left(\frac{20}{3}\right) + \left(\frac{75}{8}\right) - \left(\frac{187}{8}\right) + \left(\frac{55}{24}\right)$$

$$= \frac{(160 + 225 - 561 + 55)}{24}$$

$= -\frac{121}{24}$

$= -5\frac{1}{24}$

50. If $-12 \times (-3) + [20 \div (-4) - (-24) \div 8] - [16 \div (-2)] = (-28 \div 7) + x$, then the value of x is:

A. 29
B. 39
C. 46
D. 47

Answer: C
Explanation:
Given,
$-12 \times (-3) + [20 \div (-4) - (-24) \div 8] - [16 \div (-2)] = (-28 \div 7) + x$
$\Rightarrow -12 \times -3 + [20 \div (-4) + 24 \div 8] - [16 \div (-2)] = (-4) + x$
$\Rightarrow 36 + [(-5) + 3] - [-8] = (-4) + x$
$\Rightarrow 36 + (-2) + 8 = (-4) + x$
$\Rightarrow x = 46$

www.ingramcontent.com/pod-product-compliance
Ingram Content Group UK Ltd.
Pitfield, Milton Keynes, MK11 3LW, UK
UKHW061704190726
13853UKWH00008B/2391